Study Guide AP® Human Geography Simplified

Master essential AP® Human Geography concepts with in-depth review. Proven strategies and targeted practice questions to boost your confidence and achieve the top score on exam day

© 2024 Mastering AP® Human Geography: The Complete Prep Guide All rights reserved. This document is intended exclusively for informational use in relation to 'Mastering AP® Human Geography: The Complete Prep Guide.' The book is provided 'as is,' with no guarantees, either explicit or implied. All trademarks and brand names referenced herein are the property of their respective owners. The publisher disclaims any liability for damages that may arise from the use or improper use of the information contained within this book. Unauthorized reproduction, distribution, or transmission of this book, whether in whole or in part, is strictly forbidden.

AP® and Advanced Placement® are registered trademarks of the College Board, which was not involved in the production of, and does not endorse, this product.

Table of Contents

Introduction 6
    Overview of AP Human Geography Exam 8
        What to Expect in the Exam 9
        Scoring and Credit Benefits 10
        Study Tips for Success 11

Chapter 1: Geographic Concepts and Perspectives 13
    Subchapter 1.1: Understanding Maps and Scales 16
    Subchapter 1.2: Types of Regions 17
    Subchapter 1.3: Geographic Data and Analysis 18
        Using GIS and Remote Sensing 20

Chapter 2: Population and Migration 23
    Subchapter 2.1: Global Population Trends 26
    Subchapter 2.2: Population Distribution and Density 28
    Subchapter 2.3: Migration Patterns and Theories 30
        Push and Pull Factors 34
        Case Studies of Migration: Historical & Modern 37

Chapter 3: Cultural Patterns and Processes 41
    Subchapter 3.1: Cultural Landscapes and Identity 46
    Subchapter 3.2: Language, Religion, and Ethnicity 50
        Global Distribution 51
    Subchapter 3.3: Diffusion of Culture 53
        Contagious, Hierarchical, and Relocation Diffusion 54

Chapter 4: Political Geography 57
    Subchapter 4.1: Sovereignty and Boundaries 60

Types of Boundaries... 61

Subchapter 4.2: Geopolitical Conflicts and State Formation 63

Subchapter 4.3: Supranational Organizations and Globalization.............. 65

Chapter 5: Agriculture and Rural Land Use 68

Subchapter 5.1: Agricultural Revolutions 71

Subchapter 5.2: Global Patterns of Food Production 73

Subsistence vs. Commercial Agriculture 74

Subchapter 5.3: Environmental Impacts of Agriculture............................ 76

Chapter 6: Industrialization and Economic Development............................. 78

Subchapter 6.1: Economic Sectors (Primary, Secondary, Tertiary) 81

Subchapter 6.2: Industrial Location Theories 83

Weber's Least Cost Theory 84

Subchapter 6.3: Globalization and Economic Disparities 86

Case Studies of Newly Industrialized Countries 88

Chapter 7: Urbanization and Cities... 90

Subchapter 7.1: Urban Models (Burgess, Hoyt, Harris-Ullman) 93

Subchapter 7.2: Suburbanization and Urban Sprawl 94

Subchapter 7.3: Urban Planning and Sustainability................................. 97

Chapter 8: Human-Environment Interaction 99

Subchapter 8.1: Environmental Sustainability 101

Subchapter 8.2: Climate Change and Human Geography....................... 103

Subchapter 8.3: Adaptation and Mitigation Strategies 104

Chapter 9: Practice Questions and Case Studies 107

- Subchapter 9.1: Exam-Style Multiple Choice...................................... 111
- Subchapter 9.2: Free Response Questions (FRQ) Practice 113

    Structuring High-Scoring FRQs 113

  Subchapter 9.3: Common Pitfalls and Mistakes to Avoid 115

Chapter 10: Exam Strategy and Time Management 118

  Subchapter 10.1: Allocating Time for Each Section 120

  Subchapter 10.2: Last-Minute Study Tips 121

  Subchapter 10.3: Exam Day Tips and Strategies 122

Appendix 124

  Glossary of Key Terms 125

BONUS 127

Answers 128

Introduction

The AP® Human Geography exam is a gateway to understanding the complex patterns and processes that shape human interaction with the earth's surface. It delves into topics such as population distribution, cultural landscapes, economic development, and urbanization, offering students a comprehensive view of the world and its diverse inhabitants. This exam not only tests your knowledge of geographical concepts but also evaluates your ability to apply this knowledge to real-world scenarios, making it a valuable assessment for any student interested in the social sciences.

To excel in this exam, it's crucial to grasp the fundamental concepts of human geography and to develop the ability to think geographically. This involves understanding the spatial relationships and patterns that characterize human activity across the globe. From the migration patterns of populations to the spread of cultural practices and the development of urban spaces, human geography offers insights into the myriad ways humans interact with their environments.

One of the key challenges students face when preparing for the AP® Human Geography exam is the breadth of topics covered. The exam's comprehensive nature requires a solid understanding of various geographical concepts and the ability to analyze and interpret geographic data. This can be daunting for those new to the subject, but with the right approach, mastering these concepts is entirely achievable.

Effective preparation for the AP® Human Geography exam involves a combination of thorough review of the material, practice with exam-style questions, and the development of critical thinking skills. It's not enough to simply memorize facts; students must also be able to apply their knowledge to new situations and demonstrate their understanding of geographical principles in their answers.

In this guide, we will provide you with a structured approach to studying for the AP® Human Geography exam. We'll cover each of the key topics in detail, offering clear explanations and practical examples to help you understand complex concepts.

Additionally, we'll share proven strategies for success on the exam, including tips for tackling multiple-choice questions and writing high-scoring free-response answers.

As you embark on your study journey, remember that success in AP® Human Geography is within reach. With dedication, the right strategies, and a deep understanding of the material, you can achieve a score that reflects your hard work and commitment to mastering the subject.

Our guide is designed to build your confidence by breaking down complex topics into manageable segments, making it easier for you to absorb and retain the information. We understand that each student has a unique learning style, which is why we offer a variety of methods to study, including visual aids, interactive quizzes, and real-world examples. These tools are not only meant to enhance your understanding but also to make learning engaging and enjoyable.

To further aid in your preparation, we include essential practice questions that mirror the format and difficulty level of the actual exam. Practicing with these questions will not only test your knowledge but also improve your time management skills, a crucial aspect of exam success. We also delve into the analysis of past exam trends to give you insight into what examiners are looking for and how to approach each question strategically.

Moreover, we recognize the importance of a holistic understanding of human geography. Therefore, our guide also emphasizes the application of geographic concepts to current global issues, such as climate change, urbanization, and migration. This not only prepares you for the AP® exam but also equips you with knowledge that is applicable beyond the classroom, fostering a deeper appreciation for the subject matter.

In addition to academic preparation, we offer guidance on how to maintain a balanced study routine, manage stress, and stay motivated throughout your exam preparation journey. These tips are designed to help you navigate the challenges of exam preparation, ensuring that you remain focused and on track to achieving your goals.

Remember, the key to mastering AP® Human Geography lies in consistent study, practice, and a willingness to explore the subject in depth. By following this guide, you are taking a significant step towards not only excelling in the AP® exam but also laying a solid foundation for future academic and professional endeavors in the field of geography and beyond.

Our commitment is to provide you with all the resources and support you need to succeed. We believe in your potential and are here to guide you through every step of your AP® Human Geography exam preparation. Let's embark on this educational journey together, with the assurance that a thorough understanding of human geography and a high score on the exam are well within your reach.

Overview of AP Human Geography Exam

The AP Human Geography exam is structured to assess your comprehension and application of geographical concepts and processes. It consists of two main sections: multiple-choice questions (MCQs) and free-response questions (FRQs). The MCQ section comprises 60 questions, which accounts for 50% of your total score, and you are given 60 minutes to complete it. This section tests your ability to recognize and understand key concepts, geographical data, and their applications. The FRQ section, on the other hand, includes three questions and makes up the remaining 50% of your score, with 75 minutes allotted for completion. Here, you are evaluated on your ability to articulate complex ideas, analyze geographic issues, and synthesize information to provide coherent responses.

To excel in both sections, it is imperative to familiarize yourself with the exam format and practice extensively. For the MCQs, focus on improving your speed and accuracy by practicing with timed quizzes. Learn to identify keywords in questions to quickly ascertain what is being asked. For the FRQs, practice organizing your thoughts quickly and writing clear, concise answers. It's beneficial to outline your responses before writing to ensure that your answer is structured logically and covers all parts of the question.

Understanding the scoring criteria for the FRQs can significantly aid your preparation. Each FRQ is scored on a scale, with points awarded for demonstrating comprehensive knowledge, application of geographic concepts, and the ability to provide examples where required. Familiarize yourself with the rubric used by examiners to better understand what is expected in your responses.

Lastly, reviewing past exam questions and answers can provide insight into the types of questions asked and the level of detail expected in responses. The College Board website offers access to previous years' exams and scoring guidelines, which can be invaluable resources during your study.

By adopting a strategic approach to your exam preparation, focusing on both content knowledge and exam technique, you can enhance your confidence and performance in the AP Human Geography exam.

What to Expect in the Exam

The AP Human Geography exam is a comprehensive test that evaluates your ability to connect and apply geographic concepts to real-world scenarios. It's essential to understand the format and expectations of both the multiple-choice and free-response sections to navigate the exam confidently. The multiple-choice questions often present scenarios, maps, or data sets, requiring you to analyze and apply geographic concepts. Success in this section hinges on your ability to quickly interpret information and eliminate incorrect answers. On the other hand, the free-response section demands well-organized, detailed responses that demonstrate your understanding of geographic principles and your ability to apply them to novel situations. To excel, practice structuring your answers in a clear, logical manner, integrating specific examples to illustrate your points.

Time management is crucial during the exam. For the multiple-choice section, aim to spend no more than one minute per question, allowing extra time to review more challenging questions. In the free-response section, allocate your time based on the points each question is worth, typically spending more time on questions that carry more weight. Developing a strategy for how you approach each section can significantly impact your performance.

Familiarity with the exam's structure and types of questions asked can alleviate much of the anxiety surrounding the test. Utilize available resources such as practice exams and the College Board's website to familiarize yourself with the exam format. Engaging with these materials can also help identify areas where further review is needed, allowing you to focus your study efforts more effectively.

Remember, the AP Human Geography exam is not just about memorizing facts but understanding and applying geographic concepts to analyze the world around you. By focusing on these skills during your preparation, you can approach the exam with confidence, ready to demonstrate your geographic knowledge and critical thinking abilities.

Scoring and Credit Benefits

Achieving a high score on the AP® Human Geography exam can unlock significant academic and financial benefits, making your hard work truly worthwhile. Scores on the AP® exams range from 1 to 5, with a 5 being the highest possible score. Colleges and universities often grant course credit and placement to students who score a 3 or higher, allowing you to save on tuition fees by reducing the number of classes you need to take. This advantage can be particularly beneficial, as it may enable you to graduate earlier or allocate time and resources towards other academic or extracurricular pursuits during your college years.

Understanding the scoring system is crucial to strategize your study plan effectively. The multiple-choice section is graded by a computer, tallying correct answers without penalty for incorrect guesses, encouraging you to answer every question. On the other hand, the free-response questions are evaluated by college professors and experienced AP® teachers who apply a holistic grading method. This method assesses your ability to articulate your understanding of geographic concepts, the relevance of your examples, and the coherence of your argumentation. Familiarizing yourself with the scoring rubrics available on the College Board website can provide insights into what examiners are looking for in high-scoring responses.

To maximize your scoring potential, focus on areas that carry the most weight and align with your strengths. Practice consistently with past exam questions, paying close attention to the feedback on free-response questions to refine your writing skills and analytical thinking. Remember, achieving a high score not only reflects your mastery of the subject but also signals your readiness for college-level coursework to admissions officers.

Moreover, the confidence and skills you develop while preparing for the AP® Human Geography exam—such as critical thinking, time management, and the ability to synthesize complex information—are invaluable assets that will benefit you throughout your academic and professional life. By approaching your exam preparation with diligence and strategic planning, you are setting the stage for success, both on the exam and in your future endeavors.

Study Tips for Success

Effective study habits are essential for mastering the content of the AP® Human Geography exam and achieving a high score. One proven strategy is to **create a study schedule** that allocates specific times for reviewing each topic. This approach ensures that you cover all necessary material without becoming overwhelmed. It's important to start early and to stick to your schedule as closely as possible, allowing for flexibility when needed.

Another key to success is **active learning**. Simply reading the textbook or your notes is often not enough to deeply understand and retain the complex concepts of human geography. Engage with the material by creating flashcards, participating in study groups, and teaching the concepts to someone else. These activities promote better memory retention and understanding.

Practice exams are invaluable tools for preparation. They not only familiarize you with the exam format and types of questions but also help identify areas where you need further review. After completing each practice exam, thoroughly review your incorrect answers to understand your mistakes and learn from them.

Incorporating **visual aids** such as maps, charts, and graphs into your study routine can also enhance your learning. Many concepts in human geography are spatial and visual in nature, and these tools can help you visualize and remember patterns, processes, and data more effectively.

Lastly, **time management** during your study sessions is crucial. Use techniques such as the Pomodoro Technique, where you study intensely for short periods followed by short breaks. This method can help maintain your focus and prevent burnout. Additionally, ensure that you are balancing your study time among the various topics, giving more attention to those areas where you are weakest.

By adopting these strategies, you can build a strong foundation in AP® Human Geography, improve your exam performance, and increase your confidence. Remember, consistent effort, active engagement with the material, and effective time management are key components of exam success.

Chapter 1: Geographic Concepts and Perspectives

Understanding maps and scales is fundamental in the study of AP® Human Geography as they are the tools geographers use to interpret the world around us. Maps serve as visual representations of the earth's surface, showing physical and human-made features, while scales provide a way to measure distances and compare the sizes of different places accurately. To begin with, it's essential to grasp the concept of map scales, which can be presented in three main forms: ratio or fractional scales, written scales, and graphic scales. Each type of scale serves a specific purpose and is used in different contexts to help understand the size, distance, and layout of the geographical area being studied.

Ratio or fractional scales express the distance on a map and its corresponding distance on the earth's surface in the form of a fraction or ratio. For example, a map scale of 1:100,000 means that one unit of measurement on the map is equal to 100,000 of the same units on the ground. This type of scale is crucial when calculating actual distances between locations on a map. Written scales, on the other hand, describe the relationship between map and real-world distances in words, such as "one inch equals one mile." This form is more accessible for some as it directly states the scale without requiring conversion. Lastly, graphic scales, also known as bar scales, depict the scale of a map using a line marked with distances in the real world, providing a visual guide that can be used to measure distances directly on the map.

Maps are not just static representations of geography; they are dynamic tools that can illustrate various geographic concepts, such as the distribution of populations, cultural features, or climatic zones. They come in different types, each serving a specific purpose. Physical maps highlight natural features like rivers, mountains, and lakes, while political maps focus on man-made boundaries such as countries, states, and cities. Thematic maps are particularly useful in human geography as they can show a wide range of information, including economic activities, language distribution, religious practices, and more, often using symbols or colors to represent different data.

The ability to read and interpret maps accurately is a skill that AP® Human Geography students must develop to succeed in the exam and in their broader geographical studies. This involves not only understanding the types of maps and scales but also being able to analyze the information presented and apply it to real-world situations. For instance, examining a population density map can reveal patterns of urbanization, migration trends, or areas of potential conflict over resources. Similarly, analyzing a map showing linguistic regions can provide insights into cultural diffusion processes and the impact of historical migrations.

In addition to traditional paper maps, geographers now increasingly rely on digital mapping tools and Geographic Information Systems (GIS) to collect, analyze, and present spatial data. GIS allows for the layering of various types of data on a single map, offering a more complex and detailed view of geographical phenomena. This technology plays a crucial role in modern human geography, enabling the analysis of environmental changes, urban planning, disaster management, and much more. As we delve further into the subject, the importance of mastering these tools and understanding their applications in human geography becomes apparent.

Understanding the intricacies of Geographic Data Analysis is another cornerstone of AP® Human Geography that builds upon the foundational knowledge of maps and scales. Geographic data comes in various forms, including census data, satellite imagery, and GPS tracking, each offering unique insights into human and physical patterns on the Earth's surface. Analyzing this data requires a critical eye and the ability to discern patterns, anomalies, and trends. For example, census data can provide detailed information on population demographics, economic conditions, and housing patterns, which are essential for studying urbanization, social inequalities, or migration trends.

The use of Geographic Information Systems (GIS) and Remote Sensing has revolutionized the way geographers collect, analyze, and interpret geographic data. GIS allows for the integration and manipulation of spatial data to create detailed maps and models that can visualize complex geographic relationships and processes. Remote

Sensing, on the other hand, uses satellite or aerial imagery to gather information about the Earth's surface, enabling the study of environmental changes, land use patterns, and resource distribution without physical presence on the ground. These technologies not only enhance our understanding of geographic phenomena but also improve decision-making in areas such as urban planning, environmental management, and disaster response.

To effectively analyze geographic data, students must develop skills in spatial thinking and data interpretation. This involves recognizing the significance of location, scale, and connections between different geographic phenomena. For instance, understanding how climate change impacts migration patterns requires analyzing data from multiple sources, including weather patterns, agricultural productivity, and population movements. By synthesizing this information, students can gain insights into the complex interplay between environmental factors and human behavior.

Practice with real-world data sets and case studies is crucial for developing these analytical skills. Engaging with actual geographic scenarios allows students to apply their knowledge and understanding of maps, scales, and data analysis in a practical context. This not only prepares them for the AP® Human Geography exam but also equips them with valuable skills for future academic and professional endeavors in geography and related fields.

Moreover, the ability to communicate geographic information effectively is an essential skill for AP® Human Geography students. This includes creating clear and informative maps, graphs, and charts, as well as writing concise and coherent analyses of geographic data. Effective communication ensures that complex geographic information is accessible to a wide audience, including policymakers, researchers, and the general public, facilitating informed decision-making and fostering a greater understanding of our world.

In conclusion, mastering geographic concepts and perspectives is a multifaceted process that involves understanding maps and scales, analyzing geographic data, and utilizing modern technologies like GIS and Remote Sensing. By developing these skills, students can enhance their ability to think critically about the world around them, apply geographic knowledge to real-world situations, and communicate their findings effectively. As they progress through the AP® Human Geography course, students will discover the power of geography to explain patterns of human behavior, cultural dynamics, and environmental processes, laying the groundwork for success on the exam and beyond.

Subchapter 1.1: Understanding Maps and Scales

Maps are fundamental tools in AP® Human Geography, serving as visual representations of the earth's surface. They allow geographers to convey complex spatial information in a simplified manner. Understanding maps and scales is crucial for interpreting geographic data accurately. Maps come in various types, each designed for specific purposes. Physical maps highlight natural features like rivers and mountains, while political maps focus on boundaries, cities, and countries. Thematic maps are particularly useful in human geography, as they display specific themes or patterns, such as population density, linguistic diversity, or economic activities.

Scales are essential for understanding the level of detail a map represents. A map scale can be presented in three forms: a ratio or fraction scale, which shows the numerical relationship between distances on the map and actual distances on the ground; a graphic scale, which is a visual representation of distances; and a written scale, which describes in words the distance on the map and the corresponding distance on the ground. Grasping how to use scales is key to accurately measuring distances, understanding the extent of geographic phenomena, and comparing different regions or locations.

For students preparing for the AP® Human Geography exam, mastering the interpretation of maps and scales is not only about memorizing definitions but also about applying this knowledge to analyze geographic patterns and processes. Practice exercises might include interpreting various types of maps, calculating distances using different scales, and analyzing thematic maps to extract information about human-environment interactions, urbanization patterns, or demographic changes.

Effective strategies to enhance map-reading skills include regularly practicing with sample maps, focusing on different themes, and scales. Engage with interactive mapping tools like GIS (Geographic Information Systems) and Google Earth to get a hands-on experience with maps and scales in a digital format. These platforms offer opportunities to explore geographic data layers, analyze spatial relationships, and understand the dynamics of change over time.

Remember, maps are not just static images; they are dynamic tools that tell stories about human and physical landscapes. As you prepare for the AP® Human Geography exam, approach map-reading exercises with curiosity and critical thinking. Ask questions about what the map shows, why certain representations are used, and what insights can be gained from analyzing the map. This analytical approach will not only aid in exam preparation but also in developing a deeper understanding of the interconnectedness of the world's geographic patterns and processes.

Subchapter 1.2: Types of Regions

Understanding the types of regions is crucial for mastering AP® Human Geography. Regions help geographers categorize spaces to better understand the complexities of human activity, physical landscapes, and how they interact. There are three primary types of regions: formal, functional, and vernacular. Each type serves a unique purpose in the study of human geography and offers different insights into the spatial organization of people, cultures, and economies.

Formal regions, also known as uniform or homogeneous regions, are defined by one or more common characteristics that set them apart from surrounding areas. These characteristics can be physical, such as a mountain range, or cultural, such as a shared language or religion. Formal regions have clear, often legally recognized boundaries. Examples include the United States, the Sahara Desert, or Francophone countries where French is the primary language.

Functional regions are defined by a central point and the surrounding areas that are affected by or dependent on that central location. These regions are often organized around a key focal point, such as a city or a business, and the influence diminishes as the distance from the focal point increases. Functional regions are dynamic and can change based on the function they are centered around. Examples include the metropolitan area of New York City, the Amazon Basin, or the area served by a particular public transportation system.

Vernacular regions, also known as perceptual or cognitive regions, are defined by people's beliefs, emotions, and attitudes about a particular area. These regions do not have formal boundaries and can vary widely from person to person. They are often identified by colloquial terms or slang and reflect the cultural identity of the inhabitants. Examples include the American "Deep South," "Silicon Valley," or "The Middle East."

To effectively prepare for the AP® Human Geography exam, students should practice identifying and classifying different types of regions. Analyzing various maps and case studies can help students understand the characteristics that define each type of region and how these regions interact with one another. Consider the following practice questions to test your understanding of regions:

aggiungi altri
Understanding the nuances of these regions and their applications in human geography will enhance your ability to analyze spatial data, interpret maps, and understand the complex ways in which humans interact with their environments. Engaging with these concepts through practice questions, map analysis, and real-world applications will build a solid foundation for success on the AP® Human Geography exam.

Subchapter 1.3: Geographic Data and Analysis

In the realm of AP® Human Geography, **geographic data and its analysis** stand as pivotal components that empower students to dissect and comprehend the multifaceted nature of human and physical landscapes across the globe. This subchapter delves into the essence of geographic data, encompassing both qualitative and quantitative forms, and the methodologies employed in its analysis to unearth patterns, trends, and relationships within geographic phenomena. Geographic Information Systems (GIS) and remote sensing emerge as instrumental technologies in this endeavor, offering sophisticated tools for data collection, visualization, and interpretation.

Geographic data can be derived from a multitude of sources including census reports, satellite imagery, and field observations, each contributing a layer of insight into the spatial dynamics at play. The data encompasses a broad spectrum, from demographic statistics and economic indicators to environmental attributes and cultural patterns. The ability to navigate through this data, discerning relevant information and applying it to solve geographic queries, is a skill of paramount importance for students aiming for success in the AP® Human Geography exam.

Analysis of geographic data involves a series of steps beginning with the collection and organization of data, followed by its examination through various analytical techniques. Spatial analysis tools within GIS enable the identification of patterns such as clustering of populations or dispersion of natural resources. Moreover, thematic mapping and spatial modeling are potent techniques that facilitate the visualization of complex geographic relationships and scenarios, making them more comprehensible.

The application of **remote sensing** technology plays a crucial role in enhancing our understanding of the Earth's surface and atmosphere, offering a vantage point that is unattainable through ground-based observations alone. Through the analysis of data captured by satellites and aerial sensors, geographers can monitor environmental changes, track urban expansion, and assess the impact of natural disasters, among other applications. This capability to observe and analyze geographic phenomena from a distance is invaluable in the study of human geography.

To harness the full potential of geographic data and its analysis, students are encouraged to engage with practical exercises that involve real-world data sets and scenarios. These activities could range from analyzing population density maps to assess urban sprawl, to utilizing GIS software to model the potential impacts of climate change on coastal regions. Through hands-on experience, students not only gain proficiency in technical skills but also develop a deeper appreciation for the power of geographic data in elucidating the complex interplay between humans and their environments.

As students embark on their journey through the AP® Human Geography curriculum, it is imperative that they approach the study of geographic data and its analysis with curiosity and an analytical mindset. By mastering these skills, they equip themselves with the ability to critically evaluate geographic information, craft evidence-based arguments, and propose solutions to real-world geographic challenges. This subchapter aims to lay the foundation for such mastery, providing students with the knowledge and tools necessary to navigate the vast landscape of geographic data with confidence and acumen.

Using GIS and Remote Sensing

Geographic Information Systems (GIS) and remote sensing are not just tools but gateways to a deeper understanding of our world from a geographical perspective. These technologies allow us to collect, manage, analyze, and visualize geographic information in ways that reveal relationships, patterns, and trends in the form of maps, globes, reports, and charts. For students aiming to excel in AP® Human Geography, becoming proficient in using GIS and interpreting data from remote sensing is crucial. It equips you with the ability to analyze the spatial implications of human activities and natural processes on Earth's surface, providing a competitive edge in the exam.

GIS operates on the principle that almost all information has a geographical component. It integrates various types of data layers using spatial location as a common reference point for all the information. This could include mapping out the distribution of a certain demographic across a city, analyzing environmental data to study climate change, or even tracking the spread of diseases to understand patterns of outbreaks in relation to geography. The power of GIS lies in its ability to provide a multi-layered analysis that can visually articulate complex spatial relationships and phenomena. Engaging with GIS in your studies means you're not just looking at data; you're seeing the story behind the data, how it all connects on a geographical canvas.

Remote sensing, on the other hand, offers a bird's-eye view of the Earth's surface, providing invaluable data that can be analyzed to monitor and assess environmental changes, urban sprawl, agricultural practices, and more. It involves collecting data from satellites or aircraft to obtain information about objects or areas from a distance, without making physical contact. For example, satellite images can help track deforestation in the Amazon rainforest, measure sea surface temperatures to predict hurricane formations, or monitor urban development patterns in fast-growing cities. This technology is particularly useful in studying large-scale geographical phenomena over time, offering insights that are not possible to gather through traditional ground-based observations alone.

To effectively incorporate **GIS and remote sensing** into your AP® Human Geography studies, start by familiarizing yourself with basic GIS software. Many platforms offer free versions or trial periods for educational purposes. Experiment with adding different data layers, analyzing them, and creating your own maps. This hands-on experience will not only improve your technical skills but also deepen your understanding of geographical concepts and how they apply to real-world scenarios.

Similarly, explore online databases and libraries that provide access to remote sensing images and data. Many government and educational institutions share satellite imagery and aerial photographs that can be used for academic research. Practice interpreting these images, identifying geographical features, and understanding the implications of what you see in relation to human geography topics such as urbanization, climate change, or resource management.

Incorporating GIS and remote sensing into your study routine will transform how you perceive and analyze geographical data. It encourages a proactive approach to learning, where you're not just passively absorbing information but actively engaging with it, applying critical thinking to solve complex geographical problems. This skill is invaluable, not just for the AP® Human Geography exam but for any future academic or professional endeavors in the field of geography.

Remember, mastering these technologies is not an overnight process. It requires patience, practice, and persistence. However, the ability to visualize and analyze geographical data through GIS and remote sensing will provide a significant advantage in understanding the intricate patterns of human and physical landscapes on our planet. Engage with these tools regularly, explore various datasets, and challenge yourself with projects that push the boundaries of your geographical analysis skills. This hands-on experience will not only prepare you for the AP® Human Geography exam but also set a strong foundation for your future studies and career in geography.

Chapter 2: Population and Migration

Global Population Trends have become a focal point in understanding the dynamics of human geography. The world's population, now exceeding 7.8 billion people, continues to grow, albeit at a slowing rate. This growth is not uniform across the globe; certain regions experience rapid increases, while others face stagnation or even decline. Factors influencing these trends include fertility rates, mortality rates, and migration patterns. High fertility rates in many developing countries contrast sharply with the lower rates in more developed regions, where populations are aging. Mortality rates have declined globally due to improvements in healthcare, nutrition, and sanitation, contributing to longer life expectancies. However, disparities exist, and in some areas, particularly in sub-Saharan Africa, high mortality rates persist, often exacerbated by diseases such as HIV/AIDS.

Migration patterns further complicate population trends. People move for a myriad of reasons, including economic opportunities, political instability, environmental factors, and family reunification. These movements have significant implications for both the origin and destination regions, affecting labor markets, cultural landscapes, and demographic compositions. The phenomenon of urbanization is closely tied to migration, as people relocate from rural areas to cities in search of better living conditions and employment opportunities. This urban migration contributes to the growth of megacities, especially in Asia and Africa, and presents challenges such as housing shortages, increased demand for services, and environmental degradation.

To grasp the complexity of global population trends, it's crucial to analyze data and statistics that reveal the nuances of growth, decline, and movement. Understanding these patterns provides a foundation for studying other aspects of human geography, including cultural patterns, economic development, and environmental impact. Engaging with this topic requires not only memorizing facts but also critically evaluating the causes and consequences of population changes. Students should consider how demographic trends influence and are influenced by other geographic phenomena, creating a web of interdependencies that shapes the human experience on Earth.

Population distribution and density are key concepts in analyzing global population trends. Distribution refers to the pattern of where people live, while density measures how many people occupy a specific area. These concepts help geographers understand the spatial aspects of population, such as why certain areas are heavily populated while others remain sparsely inhabited. Factors such as climate, topography, soil fertility, and access to water significantly influence population distribution. For example, river valleys and coastal areas tend to have higher densities because they offer fertile land and access to trade routes. In contrast, deserts, high mountains, and polar regions typically have low population densities due to harsh living conditions.

The study of population distribution and density also involves examining the implications of uneven distribution. High population densities can lead to overcrowding, pollution, and strain on resources and infrastructure. Conversely, areas with low densities may struggle with economic development due to a lack of labor and markets. Policymakers and planners use insights from population geography to address these challenges, implementing strategies to manage growth, improve living conditions, and promote sustainable development.

In preparing for the AP® Human Geography exam, students should familiarize themselves with the tools and methods used to study population, such as demographic transition models, population pyramids, and migration theories. These tools offer frameworks for understanding how populations change over time and space, providing a lens through which to view the broader human geography landscape. Through careful study and analysis, students can gain a deeper appreciation for the complexity of global population trends and their far-reaching impacts on the world.

Population pyramids serve as a visual representation of a country's demographic structure, illustrating the distribution of various age groups within a population, which can provide insights into the population's growth trends, economic development stages, and social conditions. The shape of a population pyramid can indicate whether a population is expanding rapidly, as seen in many developing countries with a wide base representing a high birth rate; stable, with a more uniform distribution of age groups; or declining, where narrower bases reflect lower birth rates. These demographic structures have profound implications for planning and policy-making, affecting decisions on education, healthcare, and pensions.

Demographic transition models offer another lens through which to view population changes, describing how countries move from high birth and death rates to low birth and death rates through stages of economic development. This model helps explain the population growth patterns and the shift in population dynamics as countries progress from pre-industrial to industrialized economies. Understanding these transitions is crucial for predicting future demographic trends and addressing potential challenges related to aging populations, labor force changes, and social welfare systems.

Migration theories, including Ravenstein's Laws of Migration and Lee's Push and Pull Factors, provide frameworks for analyzing the reasons behind human migration and its effects on both origin and destination areas. These theories highlight the complexity of migration, influenced by economic opportunities, political conditions, environmental factors, and social networks. Studying these theories enables students to grasp the multifaceted nature of human movement and its implications for cultural diffusion, urbanization, and demographic diversity.

The role of urbanization in shaping demographic patterns cannot be overstated. The migration from rural to urban areas in search of better employment and living conditions has led to the rapid growth of cities around the world, transforming economic structures, social dynamics, and environmental conditions. Urbanization presents both opportunities and challenges, including economic development, cultural exchange, and innovation, alongside issues of housing, infrastructure, and sustainability. Understanding the drivers and consequences of urbanization is essential for addressing the needs of urban populations and planning for future growth.

In conclusion, mastering the concepts of population and migration is fundamental for success in the AP® Human Geography exam. By delving into global population trends, distribution and density, demographic structures, transition models, and urbanization, students equip themselves with the knowledge to analyze and interpret the complex interplay between human populations and their environments. Engaging with these topics through data analysis, case studies, and critical thinking exercises prepares students to tackle exam questions with confidence and apply geographic concepts to real-world issues. Through this comprehensive approach, students not only prepare for academic success but also gain insights into the challenges and opportunities presented by global demographic trends.

Subchapter 2.1: Global Population Trends

The examination of **global population trends** reveals a fascinating tapestry of human development and its implications on both a local and global scale. As we delve deeper into this subject, it becomes evident that understanding these trends is not just about grasping numbers but also about recognizing the underlying factors driving these changes and their potential impacts on society, economy, and the environment. **Fertility rates**, for instance, play a crucial role in shaping population growth. In many developing countries, higher fertility rates contribute to rapid population increases, presenting challenges such as strain on educational and healthcare systems, and increased demand for resources. Conversely, developed nations often face the opposite challenge with lower fertility rates leading to aging populations and the potential for a shrinking workforce, which can have profound effects on economies and social support systems.

Mortality rates have seen a global decline, thanks to advancements in healthcare, nutrition, and sanitation. This positive development has led to longer life expectancies, altering the age structure of populations worldwide. However, this achievement is not without its challenges. Aging populations require different social and healthcare services, and the shift in demographic structure can have significant economic implications, including pressures on pension systems and changes in labor market dynamics.

Migration is another critical factor influencing population trends. The movement of people across borders, whether for economic opportunities, escaping conflict, or environmental reasons, reshapes the demographic landscape of both origin and destination regions. Migration affects labor markets, cultural compositions, and even political landscapes. Urbanization, closely linked to migration, is transforming the world's cities, leading to the emergence of megacities, especially in Asia and Africa. This rapid urban growth presents both opportunities and challenges, from economic development and cultural exchange to issues of housing, infrastructure, and sustainability.

To effectively engage with the complexities of global population trends, students should consider the following strategies:

1. **Analyze demographic data**: Utilize tools like population pyramids and demographic transition models to understand the age structure and growth patterns of different populations. This analysis can provide insights into future challenges and opportunities for societies.

2. **Study migration patterns**: Investigate the causes and effects of migration, including economic, political, and environmental factors. Understanding these patterns can offer a broader perspective on global demographic changes.

3. **Examine urbanization trends**: Explore the causes and consequences of urbanization. Consider how urban growth affects economic development, social dynamics, and environmental conditions.

4. **Consider policy implications**: Reflect on how governments and international organizations might respond to demographic trends. Policies on immigration, urban planning, and social services are all influenced by changing population dynamics.

5. **Engage with case studies**: Analyze real-world examples of how countries or regions are dealing with demographic challenges. Case studies can provide valuable lessons on managing population growth, aging societies, and migration.

By adopting a multifaceted approach to studying global population trends, students can gain a deeper understanding of the forces shaping our world. This knowledge is not only crucial for excelling in the AP® Human Geography exam but also for becoming informed global citizens capable of contributing to discussions and solutions on demographic challenges facing humanity. Engaging with these topics through data analysis, critical thinking, and real-world applications prepares students to navigate the complexities of human geography with confidence and insight.

Subchapter 2.2: Population Distribution and Density

Understanding **population distribution and density** is crucial for grasping how people are spread across the earth's surface. Population distribution refers to the pattern of where people live. World population distribution is uneven; some areas are densely populated while others are sparsely populated. Factors such as climate, topography, soil fertility, and water availability significantly influence these patterns. For example, fertile plains and river valleys tend to have higher population densities because they support agriculture.

Population density is a measurement of the number of people per unit area, typically expressed per square kilometer or square mile. It provides a clearer picture of how crowded an area is. High population densities can be found in urban areas like New York City or Tokyo, where economic activities, infrastructure, and services attract more people. Conversely, arid regions such as deserts or high mountainous areas tend to have low population densities due to harsh living conditions.

To calculate population density, you divide the total population of a region by the area it occupies. This calculation helps geographers and planners understand the spatial characteristics of population distribution, plan for urban development, manage resources, and address environmental concerns. High population density can lead to challenges such as pollution, housing shortages, and traffic congestion, requiring effective planning and management strategies.

Case studies in different parts of the world illustrate how population distribution and density are influenced by environmental and human factors. For instance, the Nile River Valley in Egypt showcases how a river can create a narrow strip of fertile land in an otherwise desert region, leading to high population densities. In contrast, the Amazon Basin, despite its vast resources, has a low population density due to its dense rainforest and lack of development.

Practice questions to test your understanding:

1. What factor does not significantly affect population distribution

[A] Climate

[B] Economic opportunities

[C] Soil fertility

[D] Color of the land

2. How is population density calculated

[A] Total area / Population

[B] Total population / Total area

[C] Urban population / Rural population

[D] Land area / Water area

3. Which area is likely to have a high population density

[A] Mountainous region

[B] River valley

[C] Desert

[D] Polar region

4. What is the primary reason for urbanization in many countries

[A] Natural disasters

[B] Industrialization

[C] Agricultural advancements

[D] Cultural traditions

5. Which demographic factor is most likely to influence population growth

[A] Birth rate

[B] Death rate

[C] Migration

[D] All of the above

6. What is a common characteristic of densely populated areas

[A] Abundant natural resources

[B] High levels of pollution

[C] Low economic activity

[D] Sparse infrastructure

7. Which of the following is a consequence of high population density

[A] Increased green spaces

[B] Improved public transportation

[C] Housing shortages

[D] Lower crime rates

8. What type of land is least likely to support high population density

[A] Coastal plains

[B] Fertile valleys

[C] Arid deserts

[D] River deltas

9. Which factor can lead to population decline in a region

[A] High birth rates

[B] Outmigration

[C] Economic growth

[D] Improved healthcare

10. What is the primary method of measuring population density

[A] Population growth rate

[B] Total population / Total area

[C] Number of cities / Total area

[D] Average age of residents / Total area

Understanding these concepts is essential for analyzing human-environment interactions and planning for sustainable development. By examining population distribution and density, students can better appreciate the complexity of human geography and the challenges of managing resources and services in densely populated areas.

Subchapter 2.3: Migration Patterns and Theories

Migration is a complex phenomenon influenced by a myriad of factors that can be broadly categorized into **push and pull factors**. Push factors are conditions that drive people away from their homeland, such as economic hardships, political instability, environmental disasters, and lack of job opportunities. On the other hand, pull factors attract individuals to a new location, promising better living conditions, employment prospects, safety, and educational opportunities. Understanding these factors is crucial for analyzing migration patterns and theories that explain why and how people move from one place to another.

Theories of Migration provide frameworks to understand this movement. One of the foundational theories is the **Ravenstein's Laws of Migration**, developed in the late 19th century, which outlines patterns such as most migrants moving short distances and urban areas attracting long-distance migrants. Another significant theory is the **Gravity Model of Migration**, which suggests that larger places attract more migrants than smaller ones, and the distance between source and destination also plays a critical role in the migration decision process.

Modern theories have expanded to include the **Push-Pull Theory**, already mentioned, and the **Lee's Model of Migration**, which introduces the concept of intervening obstacles that might prevent or alter the migration process. Additionally, the **World Systems Theory** views migration as a natural consequence of global capitalism, where movements from peripheral (less developed) to core (more developed) countries are common.

Migration patterns can be **internal or international**. Internal migration involves moving within the same country or region, often from rural to urban areas, known as urbanization. International migration involves moving from one country to another and can be further classified into voluntary migration, where the move is a choice based on pull factors, and forced migration, where the move is compelled by push factors.

Case studies of migration highlight the diversity of migratory experiences. For instance, the Syrian refugee crisis showcases forced migration due to conflict, while the migration from Mexico to the United States often illustrates a mix of push (economic instability, violence) and pull (job opportunities, family reunification) factors.

Practice questions to test your understanding:

1. Which theory emphasizes the role of social networks in influencing migration decisions

[A] Gravity Model of Migration

[B] Ravenstein's Laws of Migration

[C] World Systems Theory

[D] Lee's Model of Migration

2. What is an example of chain migration

[A] A family moving from Mexico to the United States

[B] A student moving to another country for education

[C] A worker relocating to a city where relatives already reside

[D] A refugee seeking asylum in a neighboring country

3. Which of the following is a push factor in migration

[A] Job opportunities in a new country

[B] High crime rates in the home country

[C] Access to healthcare in a new location

[D] Cultural attractions in a different region

4. What term describes the movement of people from one place to another for seasonal work

[A] Internal migration

[B] Transnational migration

[C] Circular migration

[D] Permanent migration

5. Which of the following best describes the concept of remittances

[A] Money sent back home by migrants

[B] The return of migrants to their home country

[C] The process of obtaining citizenship in a new country

[D] The establishment of immigrant communities

6. What is a common reason for voluntary migration?

[A] Natural disasters

[B] Job opportunities

[C] Political persecution

[D] War

7. Which term refers to the migration of people from rural areas to urban centers?

[A] Suburbanization

[B] Urbanization

[C] Counterurbanization

[D] Exurbanization

8. What is the primary focus of the Gravity Model of Migration?

[A] Distance and population size

[B] Cultural ties

[C] Economic stability

[D] Environmental factors

9. Which of the following is an example of forced migration?

[A] A student studying abroad

[B] A family relocating for a job

[C] A refugee fleeing a war zone

[D] A retiree moving to a warmer climate

10. What does the term "brain drain" refer to in migration studies?

[A] The return of skilled workers to their home country

[B] The emigration of highly educated individuals

[C] The movement of workers to urban areas

[D] The loss of unskilled labor in a region

By dissecting the complex web of factors and theories surrounding migration, students can gain a nuanced understanding of how population movements shape and are shaped by geographic, economic, and social landscapes. This knowledge not only aids in mastering AP® Human Geography but also in developing a comprehensive perspective on global human dynamics.

Push and Pull Factors

Push and pull factors play a pivotal role in shaping migration patterns, influencing individuals and groups to move from one location to another. These factors can either compel people to leave their current residence (push factors) or attract them to a new area (pull factors). Understanding these elements is essential for grasping the complexities of migration and its impact on both origin and destination regions.

Push factors are often related to adverse conditions such as economic recession, lack of job opportunities, political instability, environmental disasters, and social discrimination. These conditions create a sense of urgency and desperation, driving individuals to seek better prospects elsewhere. For instance, areas afflicted by prolonged drought may push agricultural workers to migrate in search of more fertile lands or alternative employment opportunities.

Conversely, pull factors are characterized by the allure of better living conditions, including higher employment rates, superior education systems, political stability, and more favorable climates. Cities with booming economies, for example, pull workers from regions with fewer job opportunities, promising higher wages and improved living standards. Similarly, countries with renowned educational institutions attract students from around the globe, offering them opportunities for advancement that may not be available in their home countries.

The interplay between push and pull factors is complex and varies significantly across different contexts. For migrants, the decision to move is rarely based on a single factor; rather, it is the result of a combination of push and pull factors. Additionally, the perception of these factors can be highly subjective, influenced by individual circumstances, aspirations, and the information available to potential migrants about their prospective destinations.

To effectively analyze migration patterns, it is crucial to consider the relative strength and interaction of push and pull factors. This analysis can reveal insights into not only why people migrate but also how policies in both origin and destination countries can influence migration flows. For example, enhancing economic development and job creation in areas with high emigration rates can reduce the push factors, while strict immigration policies in destination countries might lessen the pull.

Practice questions to test your understanding:

1. Which of the following is considered a push factor in migration

[A] Advanced educational opportunities

[B] High levels of pollution

[C] Political stability

[D] Economic prosperity

2. A country with a strong economy and low unemployment rates would likely serve as a

[A] Source of emigration due to push factors

[B] Destination for immigration due to pull factors

[C] Location unaffected by migration patterns

[D] None of the above

3. How do push and pull factors work together in the migration process

[A] Push factors alone determine migration patterns

[B] Pull factors are more influential than push factors

[C] Migration is often the result of a combination of push and pull factors

[D] Push and pull factors are unrelated to the decision to migrate

4. Which of the following is an example of a pull factor that attracts migrants to a new country

[A] War and conflict

[B] Natural disasters

[C] Job opportunities

[D] Lack of resources

5. A region experiencing severe drought and famine would likely see an increase in migration due to

[A] Pull factors

[B] Push factors

[C] Neutral factors

[D] None of the above

6. Which of the following is a common push factor for refugees?
[A] Access to healthcare
[B] Political persecution
[C] Cultural diversity
[D] Economic growth

7. A city known for its vibrant job market would be considered a
[A] Source of emigration due to push factors
[B] Destination for immigration due to pull factors
[C] Location unaffected by migration patterns
[D] None of the above

8. What type of factor is often associated with natural disasters?
[A] Push factors
[B] Pull factors
[C] Neutral factors
[D] None of the above

9. Which of the following best describes a pull factor?
[A] High crime rates
[B] Availability of affordable housing
[C] Limited job opportunities
[D] Political unrest

10. A country with a high standard of living is likely to attract migrants due to
[A] Push factors
[B] Pull factors
[C] Neutral factors
[D] None of the above

By delving into the dynamics of push and pull factors, students can develop a nuanced understanding of migration. This knowledge is not only crucial for academic success in AP® Human Geography but also for fostering a comprehensive perspective on the challenges and opportunities presented by migration in the contemporary world. Through this lens, the intricate tapestry of human movement across the globe can be appreciated, revealing the underlying forces that drive one of the most fundamental aspects of human geography.

Case Studies of Migration: Historical & Modern

The Great Migration in the United States, occurring between 1916 and 1970, serves as a pivotal historical case study of internal migration. This movement saw over six million African Americans relocate from the rural Southern United States to urban centers in the North and West. The push factors included severe segregation laws known as Jim Crow laws, economic disenfranchisement, and the boll weevil infestation that devastated agricultural economies. Pull factors were the lure of industrial jobs in cities like Chicago, Detroit, and New York, which promised higher wages and a chance at a better quality of life. This migration reshaped the demographic patterns of the United States, influencing urban culture, politics, and economics. It highlights how internal migration can have profound effects on both the regions people leave and the regions to which they move.

Turning to a modern example, the Venezuelan migration crisis, which began in 2014, illustrates the complexities of contemporary migration flows. Political instability, economic collapse, and shortages of basic necessities have pushed millions of Venezuelans to leave their country, making it one of the largest external displacement crises in the world. Neighboring countries like Colombia, Brazil, and Peru have become major destinations for these migrants. This situation underscores the impact of push factors in migration and the challenges destination countries face in providing for large influxes of migrants. It also highlights the international nature of modern migration, where the effects ripple out to affect regional politics, economies, and social structures.

These case studies underscore the multifaceted nature of migration, driven by a combination of push and pull factors. They also illustrate the significant impact migration can have on individual lives, communities, and nations. For students aiming to master AP® Human Geography, understanding these case studies provides valuable insights into the dynamic processes that shape our world. It's crucial to recognize the human element in these migrations, as each number represents individual stories of hope, resilience, and the search for a better life.

Practice questions to test your understanding:

1. What was a major pull factor for African Americans during the Great Migration

[A] The availability of industrial jobs in the North

[B] The desire to return to ancestral lands

[C] The appeal of rural farming opportunities in the West

[D] The spread of Jim Crow laws to the North

2. Which of the following best describes the Venezuelan migration crisis

[A] A voluntary migration mainly for educational purposes

[B] An internal migration due to environmental disasters

[C] A forced migration due to economic and political instability

[D] A seasonal migration for agricultural work

3. How do case studies of migration like the Great Migration and the Venezuelan crisis help in understanding human geography

[A] By highlighting the impact of climate change on migration patterns

[B] By showing the effects of migration on urban and rural landscapes

[C] By illustrating the role of political policies in shaping migration flows

[D] By demonstrating the influence of economic factors on personal decisions to migrate

4. What was a significant consequence of the Great Migration on Northern cities

[A] Decreased population density in urban areas

[B] Increased cultural diversity and the establishment of vibrant communities

[C] A decline in industrial job opportunities

[D] The return of many migrants to the South

5. Which demographic group primarily participated in the Venezuelan migration crisis

[A] Young professionals seeking better job opportunities

[B] Families fleeing violence and economic hardship

[C] Retirees looking for a better quality of life

[D] Students pursuing higher education abroad

6. What role did the boll weevil infestation play in the Great Migration?

[A] It increased agricultural production in the South

[B] It caused economic hardship for Southern farmers

[C] It encouraged migration to the West

[D] It had no significant impact on migration

7. Which country has received the largest number of Venezuelan migrants?

[A] Argentina

[B] Colombia

[C] Chile

[D] Ecuador

8. What is a common challenge faced by destination countries during migration crises?

[A] Decreased job opportunities for locals

[B] Increased cultural homogeneity

[C] Overpopulation in rural areas

[D] Enhanced international relations

9. How did the Great Migration influence American music and culture?

[A] It led to the decline of jazz music

[B] It contributed to the Harlem Renaissance

[C] It had no impact on cultural movements

[D] It restricted cultural exchanges

10. What is a significant push factor in the context of migration?

[A] Availability of jobs

[B] Political stability

[C] Economic hardship

[D] Cultural acceptance

Through the examination of historical and modern migration case studies, students can gain a deeper appreciation for the complexities of human movement and its consequences. This understanding is not only academic but also fosters empathy for the challenges and decisions faced by migrants. As you continue to explore the topic of migration in AP® Human Geography, remember the power of human agency and the resilience that characterizes the migratory experience. This perspective will enrich your study and provide a solid foundation for analyzing migration patterns and their implications on a global scale.

Chapter 3: Cultural Patterns and Processes

Cultural patterns and processes are fundamental concepts in AP® Human Geography, offering insights into how cultures are formed, maintained, and transformed over time. These patterns and processes are not static; they evolve as societies interact with each other and with their environments. Understanding cultural landscapes, the visible imprint of human activity and culture on the landscape, is crucial. Every built structure, piece of farmland, city layout, and political boundary tells a story of the cultural processes at work. This section delves into the intricacies of cultural landscapes and identity, exploring how cultural traits such as language, religion, and ethnicity contribute to the formation of these landscapes.

Language is not merely a means of communication but a key element of cultural identity that shapes social interactions and unites communities. The distribution of languages across the globe reflects historical migrations, conquests, and trade patterns. For instance, the spread of English to every continent reflects the historical influence of the British Empire and the ongoing impact of American culture and economic power. Similarly, the distribution of the Spanish language in Latin America is a direct result of Spanish colonization. Language also plays a crucial role in shaping national identities and can be a source of conflict or unity within states.

Religion, another cornerstone of cultural identity, deeply influences cultural landscapes through the construction of places of worship, the observance of religious holidays, and the practice of rituals. The global distribution of major religions such as Christianity, Islam, Buddhism, and Hinduism demonstrates the historical spread of religious ideas through migration, trade, and conquest. Religious landscapes are marked by churches, mosques, temples, and shrines, each reflecting the architectural traditions and spiritual values of their communities. The role of religion in shaping cultural landscapes extends beyond the physical environment to influence laws, social practices, and daily life.

Ethnicity further complicates the cultural landscape by adding layers of identity that intersect with language and religion. Ethnic groups maintain distinct cultural practices, traditions, and sometimes languages that distinguish them from the dominant culture of a state. Ethnic landscapes are often marked by specific settlement patterns, agricultural practices, and architectural styles that reflect the group's cultural heritage. Ethnic neighborhoods in urban areas, such as Chinatowns or Little Italys, are vivid examples of how ethnic groups maintain their cultural identity while interacting with broader societal processes.

The global distribution of languages, religions, and ethnic groups is a testament to the dynamic nature of cultural diffusion. Cultures spread through a variety of mechanisms, including contagious diffusion, where cultural traits spread rapidly among individuals through direct contact; hierarchical diffusion, where cultural traits spread from a central authority or urban centers to other places; and relocation diffusion, where people move to new locations, bringing their cultural practices with them. These diffusion processes have created complex cultural mosaics around the world, where different cultures intersect, blend, and sometimes clash.

To understand the impact of cultural diffusion, consider the spread of global pop culture, facilitated by advances in technology and media. Music, movies, fashion, and food from one part of the world can quickly become popular in another, often blending with local cultural elements to create new hybrid forms. This phenomenon illustrates the interconnectedness of the world's cultures and the ongoing processes of cultural change and adaptation.

As we explore cultural patterns and processes, it's important to recognize the role of power dynamics in cultural interactions. Cultural imperialism, for example, occurs when a dominant culture forcibly spreads its cultural practices, often at the expense of local cultures. This can lead to cultural homogenization, where local cultures become increasingly similar to the dominant global culture, potentially leading to the loss of unique cultural identities and practices.

Understanding cultural patterns and processes is essential for analyzing human-environment interactions and planning for sustainable development. By examining population distribution and density, students can better appreciate the complexity of human geography and the challenges of managing resources and services in densely populated areas.

The examination of cultural diffusion and its mechanisms sheds light on the resilience and adaptability of cultural identities in the face of globalization. It is crucial to understand that while cultures are dynamic, they also possess a remarkable ability to maintain distinctiveness through practices, rituals, and the preservation of heritage sites. The resilience of cultural practices is evident in the celebration of traditional festivals, the revival of indigenous languages, and the preservation of culinary traditions, which continue to thrive alongside global influences. These practices not only contribute to the richness of the global cultural tapestry but also play a vital role in sustaining cultural diversity and fostering a sense of belonging among community members.

The concept of cultural landscape offers a unique lens through which to view the interplay between human societies and their environments. Cultural landscapes are not merely passive backdrops to human activity but are actively shaped and reshaped by cultural practices. This interaction between culture and environment is evident in agricultural practices, urban design, and land-use patterns, which reflect the values, economic conditions, and technological capabilities of a society. For instance, the terraced fields of the Andes or the intricate canal systems of the Netherlands exemplify how cultural landscapes are engineered to meet the needs of their inhabitants while reflecting their cultural heritage.

In exploring cultural patterns and processes, it is also vital to consider the role of spatial organization in shaping cultural identities. The spatial arrangement of cities, neighborhoods, and public spaces can influence social interactions, community cohesion, and the integration of different cultural groups. Urban planning and design play a significant role in facilitating cultural expression and interaction, from the layout of public parks and community centers to the zoning of cultural districts. These spaces become arenas for cultural exchange, celebration, and conflict resolution, highlighting the importance of thoughtful spatial planning in fostering inclusive and vibrant communities.

The study of cultural patterns and processes also extends to the examination of social norms, values, and institutions that govern behavior within societies. These elements of culture are transmitted through socialization processes and are reflected in legal systems, educational practices, and political structures. Understanding these underlying cultural norms is essential for grasitating the complexities of social interactions and the challenges of social cohesion in increasingly diverse societies.

Practice questions to test your understanding:

1. Which of the following best exemplifies the concept of a cultural landscape

[A] A city park designed for recreational activities

[B] Terraced agricultural fields in mountainous regions

[C] A natural landscape untouched by human activity

[D] A desert region with sparse vegetation

2. How does urban planning contribute to cultural expression

[A] By restricting public gatherings and cultural celebrations

[B] Through the design of spaces that facilitate social interaction and community events

[C] By enforcing uniform architectural styles in urban areas

[D] Through the privatization of public spaces, limiting access to certain groups

3. What role do social norms and values play in cultural patterns and processes

[A] They have no significant impact on cultural practices

[B] They dictate the economic policies of a society

[C] They influence behavior, social interactions, and the organization of society

[D] They are solely determined by technological advancements

4. Which of the following is an example of a folk culture

[A] The global popularity of fast food chains

[B] Traditional music and dance specific to a local community

[C] The use of social media for communication

[D] The architectural style of skyscrapers in major cities

5. How do globalization and cultural diffusion affect local cultures

[A] They lead to the complete eradication of local traditions

[B] They create opportunities for cultural exchange and hybridization

[C] They have no impact on local cultural practices

[D] They solely promote the dominance of one culture over others

6. What is a primary factor in the formation of cultural identity?

[A] Geographic location

[B] Economic status

[C] Political affiliation

[D] Technological advancement

7. Which of the following best describes contagious diffusion?

[A] Spread of culture through hierarchical channels

[B] Rapid spread of cultural traits through direct contact

[C] Movement of people carrying cultural practices

[D] Adoption of cultural traits by a dominant culture

8. How do festivals contribute to cultural identity?

[A] They create economic opportunities

[B] They reinforce social norms and community bonds

[C] They promote individualism over collectivism

[D] They have no significant impact on culture

9. What is an example of hierarchical diffusion?

[A] The spread of a viral dance trend on social media

[B] The introduction of a new fashion trend from a major city to smaller towns

[C] The migration of a community to a new region

[D] The blending of local cuisines with international flavors

10. How can cultural landscapes reflect economic conditions?

[A] They are solely determined by historical events

[B] They showcase the wealth and resources of a society

[C] They have no relation to economic factors

[D] They only reflect political boundaries

In delving into the intricacies of cultural patterns and processes, it becomes evident that culture is both a product of and a contributor to the complex web of human geography. By fostering an understanding of how cultural identities are formed, expressed, and transformed, students are equipped to navigate the challenges of a globalized world with empathy and insight. This exploration not only enriches their academic journey but also prepares them to engage with the world as informed and thoughtful global citizens, capable of contributing to a more inclusive and culturally diverse society.

Subchapter 3.1: Cultural Landscapes and Identity

Cultural landscapes and identity are deeply intertwined, reflecting the complex interactions between human societies and their environments. These landscapes are not merely the backdrop for cultural expression; they are an active part of how cultures define themselves, maintain traditions, and adapt to changes. The shaping of cultural landscapes involves a variety of processes, including the construction of buildings, the layout of cities, the use of land for agriculture, and the designation of sacred spaces. Each of these elements contributes to the identity of a culture, offering insights into the values, technologies, and social structures of a community.

Cultural landscapes are often categorized into three main types: designed landscapes, organically evolved landscapes, and associative cultural landscapes. Designed landscapes are those that are consciously designed and created by humans, such as gardens and parks, which reflect specific aesthetic and philosophical ideals. Organically evolved landscapes result from social, economic, administrative, and religious imperatives and are seen in the evolution of rural and urban landscapes over time. Associative cultural landscapes are significant for the religious, artistic, or cultural associations of the natural element rather than material cultural evidence, which might be insignificant or even absent.

The concept of **identity** in cultural landscapes is multifaceted, encompassing the ways in which communities identify with their surroundings, how they modify those surroundings to reflect their cultural practices, and how these practices are passed down through generations. Identity is also shaped by the interactions between different cultures, which can lead to the blending of cultural landscapes or, conversely, to the strengthening of cultural boundaries.

Language, religion, and ethnicity play critical roles in the formation of cultural landscapes. For example, the architecture of religious buildings not only provides a space for worship but also symbolizes the religious principles and aesthetic values of the community. Similarly, the layout of neighborhoods, the design of homes, and even the naming of streets can reflect the ethnic identity and historical narratives of the people who live there.

Cultural diffusion and the spread of cultural traits across landscapes are key to understanding the dynamic nature of cultural identities. Advances in technology, transportation, and communication have accelerated the process of cultural diffusion, making it easier for cultural practices, ideas, and innovations to spread across the globe. However, this process can also lead to concerns about cultural homogenization and the loss of local cultural identities.

To address these challenges, it is essential to foster an appreciation for cultural diversity and to support efforts to preserve cultural heritage. This can involve documenting and preserving traditional practices, supporting the use of indigenous languages, and promoting the conservation of historic sites and landscapes. Engaging with and learning from diverse cultures can enrich our understanding of the world and help to build more inclusive societies.

Practical steps for preserving cultural landscapes and identities include:
- Supporting local artisans and craftspeople whose work reflects traditional practices and contributes to the cultural landscape.
- Participating in or supporting cultural festivals and events that celebrate and educate about cultural heritage.
- Advocating for policies that protect historic sites and landscapes from development or degradation.

- Engaging in community planning processes to ensure that development respects and integrates cultural heritage.

Reflecting on cultural landscapes and identity offers a powerful lens through which to view the complexities of human interaction with the environment. It challenges us to consider not only the physical manifestations of culture but also the intangible elements that give places their unique character and meaning. By understanding and appreciating the diversity of cultural landscapes, we can better appreciate the richness of human culture and the importance of preserving it for future generations.

Practice questions to test your understanding:

1. Identify a landscape formed organically
[A] Botanical garden
[B] Town on trade route
[C] Untouched national park
[D] Sacred natural site

2. How does identity connect to cultural landscapes?
[A] Reflects designer's identity
[B] Mirrors and influences cultural practices
[C] Based on financial value
[D] Insignificant in analysis

3. How to protect cultural landscapes?
[A] Promote rapid urban growth
[B] Support local artisans with traditional methods
[C] Replace customs with modern practices
[D] Discourage preservation of customs and languages

4. What role do cultural landscapes play in community identity?
[A] They are solely for tourism
[B] They foster a sense of belonging and pride
[C] They have no impact on identity
[D] They are only historical artifacts

5. Which of the following is a consequence of neglecting cultural landscapes?

[A] Increased community engagement

[B] Loss of historical and cultural significance

[C] Enhanced tourism opportunities

[D] Strengthened local traditions

6. What is a characteristic of designed landscapes?

[A] Evolved through natural processes

[B] Created with specific aesthetic goals

[C] Primarily agricultural in nature

[D] Lacking human influence

7. How can cultural diffusion impact local identities?

[A] It leads to cultural isolation

[B] It promotes cultural blending

[C] It has no effect on identity

[D] It solely benefits tourism

8. Which element is essential for preserving cultural heritage?

[A] Ignoring traditional practices

[B] Supporting indigenous languages

[C] Promoting uniformity in culture

[D] Discouraging community involvement

9. What is a potential risk of cultural homogenization?

[A] Strengthened local traditions

[B] Increased cultural diversity

[C] Loss of unique cultural identities

[D] Enhanced global understanding

10. How do sacred spaces contribute to cultural identity?

[A] They are irrelevant to community values

[B] They symbolize shared beliefs and practices

[C] They are only for historical reference

[D] They have no impact on social structures

Subchapter 3.2: Language, Religion, and Ethnicity

Delving into the intricate web of language, religion, and ethnicity, it's crucial to recognize how these elements not only define individual and group identities but also shape cultural landscapes across the globe. Language acts as a powerful tool for communication, embodying cultural heritage and influencing social interactions. It's fascinating to observe how linguistic diversity can reveal historical migrations and conquests, with some languages spreading widely to become lingua francas in certain regions, while others remain confined to small, isolated communities, often at risk of extinction. The preservation of minority languages is vital, as each language carries unique knowledge and perspectives.

Religion, intertwined with language, plays a pivotal role in shaping cultural practices and worldviews. It can unite large groups of people or divide them, sometimes even leading to geopolitical conflicts. The global distribution of major religions—Christianity, Islam, Hinduism, Buddhism, and others—illustrates historical patterns of diffusion, conquest, and conversion. Understanding the core beliefs and practices of these religions, as well as recognizing the diversity within them, is essential for grasping their impact on cultural landscapes and social norms.

Ethnicity, closely linked to language and religion, contributes to the rich mosaic of human society. Ethnic groups share common ancestry, cultural traditions, language, or religion, which fosters a strong sense of belonging and identity. The distribution of ethnic groups across the globe is the result of complex historical migrations, empires, and social changes. Ethnic diversity can enrich societies, bringing a variety of perspectives and cultural practices. However, it can also lead to tensions and conflicts, especially in regions where ethnic boundaries do not align with political ones.

To truly understand the dynamics of human geography, one must delve into the specifics of how language, religion, and ethnicity interact with each other and with other geographic factors. For instance, examining how the French language has spread beyond Europe, influencing cultures and societies in Africa, the Americas, and the Pacific, or how the spread of Islam has shaped cultural and political landscapes in the Middle East, North Africa, and beyond. Similarly, exploring the ethnic mosaic of a country like the United States, with its history of immigration and cultural exchange, can provide insights into the challenges and opportunities of multiculturalism.

In summary, language, religion, and ethnicity are fundamental components of cultural patterns and processes, each contributing to the unique tapestry of human geography. Understanding these elements in depth allows us to appreciate the complexity of cultural identities and the ways in which they influence interactions at both local and global scales. As we continue to explore these themes, remember the importance of empathy and open-mindedness in appreciating the diverse ways in which people across the world express their identities and organize their societies.

Global Distribution

Global distribution of languages, religions, and ethnicities presents a fascinating mosaic that is constantly evolving due to migration, globalization, and the influence of technology. The spread of languages across continents can often trace the paths of historical empires and trade routes. For example, the widespread use of English in North America, Australia, and parts of Africa and Asia reflects the colonial history of the British Empire. Similarly, the distribution of Spanish and Portuguese in Latin America points to the colonial activities of Spain and Portugal. These languages serve as lingua francas in regions far from their places of origin, facilitating communication and often becoming the primary language of education and government.

Religions, too, have spread far from their birthplaces, shaping societies in profound ways. The global reach of Christianity, from Europe to the Americas, Africa, and parts of Asia, illustrates the role of missionaries and colonial powers in its dissemination. Islam's presence in North Africa, the Middle East, and parts of Asia and Europe underscores the historical spread through conquests, trade, and the pilgrimage routes. Hinduism, while predominantly practiced in India and Nepal, has diaspora communities worldwide, showing patterns of migration and the spread of cultural practices.

Ethnic diversity within countries often mirrors patterns of migration, conquest, and colonial history. The United States exemplifies a "melting pot" of ethnicities from around the globe, each contributing to the cultural fabric of the nation. Similarly, countries like Brazil, with its mix of Indigenous, Portuguese, African, and more recent Japanese influences, showcase the complex interplay of ethnicity over time.

Understanding the global distribution of languages, religions, and ethnicities requires examining the forces that drive migration and the barriers that individuals and groups face. Economic opportunities, political conflicts, environmental changes, and social networks play significant roles in shaping migration patterns. The push and pull factors, such as escaping conflict or persecution and seeking better economic conditions, are crucial for understanding these movements.

In addressing the challenges of cultural integration and preservation, it is essential to foster policies and practices that value diversity and promote inclusivity. Education systems that teach multiple languages and histories can cultivate an appreciation for cultural diversity. Policies that protect minority rights and promote social inclusion are vital for maintaining social cohesion in increasingly diverse societies.

For students preparing for the AP Human Geography exam, grasitating these concepts involves not just memorizing facts but also understanding the dynamic interactions between human societies and their environments. Engaging with case studies, current events, and interactive mapping tools can bring these concepts to life. Practice questions might explore the reasons behind the spread of a particular language or religion, the impact of migration on ethnic composition, or the challenges and opportunities of multicultural societies.

By examining the global distribution of languages, religions, and ethnicities, students gain insights into the complex tapestry of human society and the forces that shape our world. This understanding is crucial for navigating the challenges of the 21st century, marked by globalization, migration, and the need for intercultural communication and cooperation.

Subchapter 3.3: Diffusion of Culture

The diffusion of culture is a dynamic process that significantly influences human geography. It involves the spreading of cultural beliefs, practices, and innovations across different societies and landscapes. This phenomenon can occur through various means such as migration, trade, warfare, and the more contemporary modes of communication like the internet and social media. Understanding the mechanisms behind cultural diffusion is crucial for grasping the complexities of global cultural patterns and their impacts on societies.

Contagious diffusion is one of the primary forms, where cultural elements spread outward from their origin to new areas through direct contact among people. This form of diffusion is akin to the ripple effect seen when a stone is thrown into a pond. An example of contagious diffusion is the spread of agricultural practices from their places of origin to adjacent areas, eventually reaching most parts of the world.

Hierarchical diffusion involves the spread of culture from one key person or node of authority or power to other persons or places. It often skips over wider areas to target specific nodes that are more likely to adopt the innovation. The spread of fashion trends from major cities like New York or Paris to other parts of the world is a classic example of hierarchical diffusion.

Relocation diffusion occurs when people move from their original location to new places, bringing their cultural practices with them. This form of diffusion has played a significant role in the spread of various languages and religions. The migration of people from Europe to the Americas over the centuries has resulted in the relocation diffusion of Christianity, which now has a significant presence in the Western Hemisphere.

Each of these diffusion processes contributes to the shaping of cultural landscapes and the formation of cultural regions. These regions can be identified based on the prevalence of certain cultural practices, languages, or religious beliefs that have spread through one or more of the diffusion processes.

To fully appreciate the impact of cultural diffusion, consider the global spread of English. Originally spoken in England, it has become the world's lingua franca due to the British Empire's historical colonization and the contemporary influence of American culture and technology. This has led to English being adopted as a second language in many countries, influencing local cultures and facilitating global communication.

Another poignant example is the diffusion of technology, such as smartphones and social media platforms, which have rapidly spread across the globe, transforming communication patterns, social interactions, and even political movements. These technologies have enabled cultures to interact more directly and quickly than ever before, leading to an acceleration of cultural diffusion.

In studying these examples, students should analyze the factors that facilitate or hinder the diffusion of cultural elements, including physical barriers, cultural resistance, and the role of technology. They should also consider the implications of cultural diffusion for identity, cultural diversity, and conflict.

To engage with these concepts, students can explore case studies that illustrate the effects of cultural diffusion on societies. They might examine how the spread of a particular technology has influenced cultural practices in different regions or how the migration of people has led to the blending of cultures.

Understanding cultural diffusion is essential for anyone looking to grasp the complexities of human geography. It highlights the interconnectedness of the world's cultures and the ways in which cultural practices evolve and spread, shaping the world in which we live. By examining the mechanisms and effects of cultural diffusion, students can gain insights into the dynamic processes that drive cultural change and the development of cultural landscapes.

Contagious, Hierarchical, and Relocation Diffusion

The processes of contagious, hierarchical, and relocation diffusion are not just abstract concepts but are vividly demonstrated in the cultural shifts and movements we observe around the world. These mechanisms of diffusion play a crucial role in the spread of innovations, traditions, and practices, shaping societies in profound ways. Understanding these processes can empower students to analyze and predict cultural changes, offering insights into the dynamics of human interaction and the evolution of communities.

Contagious diffusion, for example, can be observed in the rapid spread of digital innovations. Social media trends, memes, and online challenges often start in a specific location or community and spread globally within days or even hours, illustrating how ideas and behaviors can proliferate through direct contact in our interconnected world. This form of diffusion underscores the importance of networks and connections in spreading cultural elements, highlighting the role of modern technology in accelerating cultural exchange.

Hierarchical diffusion is evident in the adoption of technological devices, where new products are first adopted by influential cities or social groups before trickling down to the broader population. The latest smartphone models, for instance, are often first seen in the hands of tech influencers and celebrities before becoming widespread. This pattern reflects the significance of social hierarchies and the influence of key individuals or groups in disseminating innovations.

Relocation diffusion is vividly illustrated by the global spread of cuisines. As people migrate, they bring their culinary traditions with them, introducing new flavors and dishes to their host communities. The prevalence of Italian, Chinese, and Mexican restaurants across the United States is a testament to this form of diffusion, showcasing how migration contributes to cultural diversity and enrichment.

To grasp these concepts more concretely, students can engage with interactive activities such as mapping the spread of a particular music genre or fashion trend, analyzing the role of influencers in hierarchical diffusion, or studying the impact of migration on local food cultures. These exercises not only reinforce understanding but also highlight the relevance of cultural diffusion in everyday life.

Moreover, students can benefit from examining case studies that illustrate the consequences of diffusion, both positive and negative. For instance, the global spread of fast food has had significant cultural and health implications, while the diffusion of renewable energy technologies offers solutions to global environmental challenges. Through such analyses, students can appreciate the complex interplay between culture, technology, and society, gaining a nuanced understanding of human geography.

In preparing for the AP Human Geography exam, it is crucial for students to not only memorize the definitions of contagious, hierarchical, and relocation diffusion but also to apply these concepts to real-world scenarios. Practice questions might include analyzing the spread of a technological innovation using the three types of diffusion or evaluating the impact of a cultural practice that has spread globally. Such questions encourage critical thinking and application of knowledge, skills that are invaluable for academic success and beyond.

By delving into the mechanisms of cultural diffusion, students uncover the layers of human connection and influence that shape our world. This exploration fosters a deeper appreciation for the diversity of human experiences and the shared processes that unite us across cultures and geographies. Engaging with these concepts prepares students not only for academic achievement but also for active, informed participation in a global society.

Chapter 4: Political Geography

The concept of sovereignty and boundaries is central to understanding political geography. Sovereignty refers to the authority of a state to govern itself or another state, encompassing the right to exercise its powers without external interference. This concept is foundational to the international system of states and is crucial for maintaining order and stability within and among nations. Boundaries, on the other hand, are the defined lines that mark the extent of a state's territory and its jurisdiction over the people and properties within. These lines can be physical, such as rivers, mountains, or walls, or they can be imaginary, drawn through negotiations or conflicts. The establishment and recognition of boundaries are vital for the smooth functioning of states, as they determine the geographical limits within which state laws apply and government authority is recognized.

Boundaries are not just lines on a map; they have profound implications for the identity, economy, and security of states. They can influence national identity by demarcating the space within which a shared sense of belonging and community is fostered. Economically, boundaries affect trade, resource distribution, and control over strategic areas. Security-wise, they are crucial for defense and the prevention of unauthorized entry. The process of boundary-making, known as delimitation, and the marking of these boundaries on the ground, known as demarcation, are complex and often contentious tasks that can lead to disputes and conflicts between neighboring states.

Types of boundaries include geometric, which are straight lines drawn without regard to the physical and cultural features of the land; physical-political, which align with significant features of the natural landscape like rivers or mountain ranges; and cultural-political, which align with patterns of ethnicity, language, or religion. Each type of boundary has its own set of challenges and implications for the states it separates. For instance, geometric boundaries might ignore the cultural cohesion of a community by splitting it between two states, while physical-political boundaries might create challenges for access and control of natural resources.

The concept of sovereignty and the establishment of boundaries are deeply intertwined with the notion of territoriality, which is the attempt by an individual or group to affect, influence, or control people, phenomena, and relationships by delimiting and asserting control over a geographic area. This territoriality can be seen in the way states exercise control over their territory and the people within it, asserting sovereignty and establishing boundaries to demarcate their domain. Territorial disputes arise when states claim overlapping areas or when the boundaries do not reflect the current realities of the people living in those areas. These disputes can lead to conflicts, negotiations, and, in some cases, international arbitration to resolve.

Understanding the dynamics of sovereignty, boundaries, and territoriality is essential for grasping the complexities of political geography. These concepts not only define the physical and political landscape of the world but also influence the interactions between states, the movement of people and goods, and the global distribution of power and resources. As we delve deeper into the intricacies of political geography, it becomes clear that the drawing of a boundary line on a map encapsulates a multitude of political, economic, and social considerations that shape the lives of those living within and around those lines.

Geopolitical conflicts often emerge as a direct consequence of the issues surrounding sovereignty and boundaries. These conflicts can manifest in various forms, from territorial disputes to broader struggles for political and economic control. The history of the 20th and 21st centuries provides numerous examples of such conflicts, where the drawing or redrawing of boundaries has led to wars, the displacement of populations, and long-standing hostilities between nations. The Israel-Palestine conflict, for instance, highlights the complexities of establishing recognized boundaries that satisfy the demands for sovereignty and self-determination of different groups. Similarly, the conflict in Kashmir between India and Pakistan underscores how colonial legacies, religious identities, and territorial claims can intertwine, leading to protracted disputes and violence.

State formation is another critical aspect of political geography, involving the processes through which new states are created and recognized on the global stage. The decolonization period after World War II saw a surge in state formation, as territories gained independence from European colonial powers. This process, however, was not without its challenges, as newly formed states had to navigate the complexities of establishing governance structures, defining boundaries, and securing international recognition. The breakup of the Soviet Union in the early 1990s further illustrates the dynamics of state formation, as it led to the emergence of multiple new states, each with its own challenges related to identity, sovereignty, and territorial integrity.

Supranational organizations play a pivotal role in shaping the political geography of the world. These entities, which include the United Nations, the European Union, and the African Union, among others, transcend national boundaries, allowing member states to cooperate on issues ranging from economic development to security and environmental protection. The European Union, in particular, exemplifies how supranational organizations can influence political geography by promoting economic integration, political cooperation, and a shared identity among diverse nations. However, the rise of supranational organizations also raises questions about sovereignty and the extent to which member states cede control over certain aspects of their governance to achieve broader objectives.

Globalization has further complicated the landscape of political geography by diminishing the importance of physical boundaries in some respects while reinforcing them in others. On one hand, the flow of goods, services, information, and people across borders has increased interconnectedness and interdependence among states. On the other hand, globalization has also led to the reinforcement of boundaries, as states seek to regulate immigration, protect domestic industries, and maintain national security in a rapidly changing world. The tension between the forces of globalization and the traditional concept of state sovereignty highlights the evolving nature of political geography in the 21st century.

In conclusion, the study of political geography encompasses a wide range of topics, from the foundational concepts of sovereignty and boundaries to the complexities of geopolitical conflicts, state formation, supranational organizations, and globalization. Each of these elements contributes to our understanding of the political organization of space and the ways in which power is exercised and contested on the global stage. As students delve into these topics, they gain valuable insights into the forces that shape our world, preparing them to engage with the challenges and opportunities of an increasingly interconnected global community.

Subchapter 4.1: Sovereignty and Boundaries

The delineation and management of boundaries are critical in the assertion of sovereignty, directly impacting a nation's ability to govern and exercise authority within its territorial confines. This process involves intricate negotiations and, at times, international arbitration to settle disputes that arise from overlapping claims. The establishment of boundaries is not merely a political act but also a cultural and economic one, influencing trade, security, and the social fabric of border communities. For instance, the creation of a boundary can disrupt traditional trade routes, separate communities, or even lead to the creation of new economic zones that can either benefit or disadvantage the local populations. It's essential to understand that the drawing of boundaries is a dynamic process, subject to changes due to environmental shifts, such as the changing course of a river, or political changes, like the dissolution of a country.

Types of Boundaries play a significant role in the political geography landscape, each with its unique set of challenges and considerations. **Geometric boundaries**, often seen as straight lines on a map, may seem arbitrary but are the result of detailed negotiations and agreements. These boundaries can sometimes lead to disputes when they ignore the cultural or physical landscape of an area. **Physical-political boundaries**, which align with natural features like rivers and mountain ranges, may change over time due to natural processes, necessitating periodic reevaluation and adjustment. **Cultural-political boundaries** reflect the distribution of cultural traits such as language and religion and can be particularly contentious when they fail to align with the self-identified regions of cultural groups, leading to calls for autonomy or independence.

The concept of **Territoriality** is closely linked to sovereignty and boundaries, embodying the efforts by a state to control space and influence the actions that take place within its borders. This control is not only a matter of political power but also of cultural significance, as it involves the regulation of trade, migration, and the flow of information. Territorial disputes are often deeply rooted in historical claims, economic interests, and cultural connections to the land. Resolving these disputes requires a deep understanding of the underlying issues and a commitment to finding solutions that respect the rights and needs of all parties involved.

In the context of **Globalization**, the traditional concepts of sovereignty and boundaries are being challenged. The flow of goods, services, people, and information across borders has created a new dynamic, where states must balance the benefits of open borders with the need to maintain control over their territory and protect their citizens' interests. This balance is delicate and often contested, as seen in debates over immigration policy, trade agreements, and environmental regulation.

For students preparing for the AP Human Geography exam, grasitating these concepts involves not just memorizing facts but also understanding the dynamic interactions between human societies and their environments. Engaging with case studies, current events, and interactive mapping tools can bring these concepts to life. Practice questions might explore the reasons behind the establishment of a particular boundary, the impact of migration on cultural boundaries, or the challenges of managing transboundary environmental resources.

By examining the mechanisms and effects of sovereignty and boundaries, students can gain insights into the complex processes that shape our world. This understanding is crucial for navigating the challenges of the 21st century, marked by globalization, migration, and the need for intercultural communication and cooperation. Engaging with these concepts prepares students not only for academic achievement but also for active, informed participation in a global society.

Types of Boundaries

Understanding the **types of boundaries** is crucial for mastering the AP® Human Geography exam, especially when delving into political geography. Boundaries, the invisible lines that define the territorial limits of states, vary significantly in their formation, function, and implications. These demarcations are not just physical barriers but also carry deep geopolitical, cultural, and historical significance.

Geometric boundaries are drawn based on latitude and longitude lines, often without consideration for natural or cultural features. This type of boundary is straightforward in its creation but can lead to disputes when it divides groups with strong cultural ties or splits natural resources unequally between nations.

Physical (Natural) boundaries, on the other hand, are based on recognizable natural features such as rivers, mountain ranges, or deserts. These boundaries are generally more stable and less contested, as the natural landscapes they follow can serve as a clear division. However, changes in the environment, such as river course alterations due to erosion, can challenge the permanence of these borders.

Cultural boundaries reflect human factors such as language, religion, and ethnicity. These boundaries can be particularly contentious, as they often overlap with areas of mixed populations and can lead to conflicts when political borders do not align with cultural divisions. Understanding the distribution and interaction of cultural groups is essential for analyzing these types of boundaries.

Antecedent boundaries are established before the present-day human landscape developed, meaning they do not consider the cultural or ethnic compositions of the area. These can lead to situations where diverse communities are encompassed within a single state's borders, potentially causing internal strife.

Subsequent boundaries are drawn after the development of the cultural landscape. They aim to accommodate cultural, ethnic, or economic differences but can also result from conflict and subsequent treaties. These boundaries are more likely to reflect the current realities of the regions they divide but may also be sources of tension if populations feel misrepresented.

Superimposed boundaries are imposed by external powers, often without regard for existing cultural or political landscapes. This type was particularly common during the colonial era, where European powers divided up territories with little consideration for indigenous cultures. These boundaries can lead to fragmented nations and enduring regional conflicts.

Relic boundaries are no longer functional but have left a lasting impact on the landscape or cultural consciousness. An example would be the Berlin Wall, which no longer exists as a physical barrier but whose influence persists in the urban layout and cultural memory of Berlin.

For students aiming to excel in the AP® Human Geography exam, it is vital to grasp the complexities surrounding these types of boundaries. Recognizing the historical context, current implications, and potential future changes of political borders can provide deep insights into the nature of international relations, national sovereignty, and local identities. Engaging with case studies, such as the creation of South Sudan or the disputes in the South China Sea, can offer practical examples of how boundary types influence global and regional dynamics. By analyzing these real-world scenarios, students can develop a nuanced understanding of how geographical concepts apply beyond the textbook, preparing them for both the exam and a broader comprehension of the world's political geography.

Subchapter 4.2: Geopolitical Conflicts and State Formation

In the complex world of **geopolitical conflicts and state formation**, understanding the historical and contemporary forces at play is crucial for any student aiming to master AP® Human Geography. The formation of states, often a direct consequence of geopolitical conflicts, involves processes that are deeply intertwined with issues of power, culture, and economics. These conflicts can arise from a variety of sources including, but not limited to, territorial disputes, ethnic divisions, and colonial legacies. As we delve into this topic, it's important to recognize the role of **nationalism** in state formation. Nationalism, a sense of shared identity and purpose within a population, can drive movements for self-determination and independence, leading to the creation of new states. This was evident in the breakup of the Soviet Union, where nationalist movements in countries like Estonia, Latvia, and Lithuania led to their re-emergence as independent nations.

Another pivotal aspect to consider is the impact of **colonialism** on geopolitical boundaries and state formation. The arbitrary borders drawn by colonial powers, without regard for ethnic or cultural divisions, have sown seeds of conflict in many regions, such as in Africa and the Middle East. The decolonization process, while freeing nations from colonial rule, often left behind a legacy of political instability and territorial disputes.

Supranational organizations play a significant role in mediating geopolitical conflicts and supporting the process of state formation. Organizations like the United Nations (UN) and the European Union (EU) provide platforms for negotiation and conflict resolution, offer economic support to newly formed states, and promote principles of sovereignty and territorial integrity. The recognition of a state by the international community, often facilitated by these organizations, is a critical step in the state formation process.

Economic factors cannot be overlooked when analyzing geopolitical conflicts and state formation. The control of resources, access to trade routes, and economic sanctions are tools often used in geopolitical strategies. Economic disparities and competition for resources can fuel conflicts but also create opportunities for cooperation and development, influencing the formation and stability of states.

Case studies such as the creation of South Sudan, the ongoing conflict in Syria, and the tensions in the South China Sea provide real-world examples of how geopolitical conflicts can lead to new state formations or alter the political landscape. These case studies highlight the complexity of state formation in the context of international law, ethnic and cultural identities, and global power dynamics.

For students preparing for the AP® Human Geography exam, it's essential to approach the study of geopolitical conflicts and state formation with a critical and analytical mindset. Engaging with a variety of sources, including academic texts, news articles, and international treaties, can provide a comprehensive understanding of the subject. Additionally, practicing with exam-style questions that cover these topics can help solidify knowledge and build confidence.

Strategies for success on the exam include developing a strong foundation in the key concepts of political geography, staying informed about current geopolitical events, and being able to apply theoretical knowledge to real-world scenarios. Remember, understanding the forces that shape our world is not just about preparing for an exam; it's about becoming an informed and engaged global citizen.

Subchapter 4.3: Supranational Organizations and Globalization

Supranational organizations are key players in the realm of globalization, affecting political, economic, and social landscapes across the globe. These entities, such as the United Nations (UN), the European Union (EU), the World Trade Organization (WTO), and the North Atlantic Treaty Organization (NATO), transcend national boundaries to promote cooperation, peace, economic development, and security among member states. Their influence on globalization is profound, facilitating the flow of goods, services, capital, and labor across borders, and promoting cultural exchange and understanding.

Globalization has accelerated in recent decades, driven by advancements in technology, communication, and transportation. This interconnectedness, while fostering economic growth and cultural exchange, also presents challenges such as environmental degradation, economic inequality, and the erosion of local cultures and traditions. Supranational organizations play a pivotal role in addressing these challenges, offering platforms for dialogue, negotiation, and the implementation of policies aimed at sustainable development and the equitable distribution of globalization's benefits.

The impact of supranational organizations on **political geography** is significant. By providing mechanisms for conflict resolution and cooperation, they have the potential to reduce geopolitical tensions and support the stability of international relations. For instance, the EU's role in integrating European countries through economic and political bonds has contributed to a period of unprecedented peace in a region once plagued by wars. Similarly, the UN's peacekeeping missions around the world aim to prevent conflicts and facilitate the conditions necessary for peace and development.

Economic development is another area where supranational organizations have a substantial impact. Through entities like the World Bank and the International Monetary Fund (IMF), resources are mobilized to support development projects and economic reforms in developing countries. These efforts aim to reduce poverty, enhance education, and improve infrastructure, which are essential for sustainable development and integration into the global economy.

However, the influence of supranational organizations is not without controversy. Critics argue that these bodies can infringe upon national sovereignty and that their policies may favor wealthier nations or corporations at the expense of poorer countries. The debate over the benefits and drawbacks of globalization and the role of supranational organizations in shaping it is a critical topic for students of AP Human Geography to explore.

Understanding the dynamics of supranational organizations and globalization requires examining case studies that highlight their successes and challenges. For example, analyzing the EU's handling of the eurozone crisis, the WTO's role in trade disputes, or the UN's effectiveness in peacekeeping and humanitarian missions can provide valuable insights. These case studies not only illustrate the complexities of international relations and economics but also help students grasp the real-world applications of the concepts they study.

For those preparing for the AP Human Geography exam, it's essential to understand the key functions and objectives of major supranational organizations, as well as the impacts of globalization on different regions and populations. Engaging with this topic through a variety of resources, including academic articles, news reports, and official documents from the organizations themselves, can enrich one's understanding and provide a solid foundation for exam success.

In conclusion, the study of supranational organizations and globalization is integral to understanding contemporary political geography. By examining the roles these entities play in fostering cooperation, addressing global challenges, and shaping the economic and political landscapes, students can gain a deeper appreciation of the interconnected world we live in. Through critical analysis and engagement with case studies, students can navigate the complexities of these topics, preparing them not only for the AP Human Geography exam but for informed citizenship in a globalized world.

Chapter 5: Agriculture and Rural Land Use

Agriculture and rural land use are foundational elements in the study of human geography, reflecting the diverse ways in which human societies interact with the Earth's landscapes to produce food, fiber, and other resources. The evolution of agricultural practices over time has been influenced by a variety of factors including technological advancements, cultural practices, and environmental conditions. Understanding these dynamics is crucial for anyone looking to master AP® Human Geography, as it provides insight into the economic, social, and environmental implications of agriculture on a global scale. The first agricultural revolution, which marked the transition from nomadic hunting and gathering to settled farming practices, initiated the development of more complex societies and the eventual rise of cities. This pivotal change in human history underscores the importance of agriculture in shaping human development.

As we delve deeper into the subject, it becomes apparent that agriculture's impact extends beyond the mere production of food. It plays a significant role in determining settlement patterns, land use, and economic structures in rural areas. For instance, the introduction of the Green Revolution in the mid-20th century brought about significant increases in agricultural production through the use of new technologies, high-yield crop varieties, and chemical fertilizers. However, these advancements also led to environmental challenges and socio-economic disparities, highlighting the complex relationship between agricultural practices and sustainable development.

In exploring the global patterns of food production, it's important to distinguish between subsistence and commercial agriculture. Subsistence agriculture is practiced primarily to meet the needs of the farmer's family, with little to no surplus for trade. This form of agriculture is common in parts of the world where industrialization is less advanced, and it often relies on traditional methods and local knowledge. On the other hand, commercial agriculture is characterized by large-scale production intended for widespread distribution and sale. This type of agriculture is heavily mechanized and requires significant investment in technology, infrastructure, and market access.

The environmental impacts of agriculture are profound and multifaceted. Agricultural activities can lead to deforestation, soil degradation, water scarcity, and biodiversity loss, among other issues. These challenges necessitate a careful consideration of sustainable farming practices that can mitigate negative environmental impacts while ensuring food security for the growing global population. Strategies such as integrated pest management, organic farming, and agroforestry are gaining traction as viable alternatives to conventional agricultural methods, offering hope for a more sustainable and equitable food system.

As we continue to explore the intricacies of agriculture and rural land use, it becomes clear that these topics are not only central to understanding human geography but also critical to addressing some of the most pressing challenges facing our world today. From the role of agriculture in driving economic development to its impact on environmental sustainability, the study of agricultural geography provides valuable insights into the complex interactions between humans and the planet.

The exploration of agricultural revolutions reveals a timeline of innovation and adaptation that has profoundly shaped human societies. The Second Agricultural Revolution, coinciding with the Industrial Revolution, introduced mechanized farming equipment and improved crop rotation techniques, significantly boosting productivity and supporting urban population growth. The Green Revolution further accelerated agricultural output with the development of high-yield crop varieties and expanded use of chemical fertilizers and pesticides. While these revolutions have enabled unprecedented levels of food production, they also underscore the critical need for sustainable practices in the face of environmental and social challenges.

Global patterns of food production are influenced by a complex interplay of physical geography, technology, and policy. Regions such as the Midwest in the United States, the Pampas in Argentina, and the Indo-Gangetic Plain in India have become agricultural heartlands, thanks to fertile soils, favorable climates, and investments in agricultural infrastructure and technology. These areas exemplify the shift towards commercial agriculture, which dominates in developed countries and increasingly in developing economies. The global trade network for agricultural commodities ties these disparate regions together, creating a web of economic interdependence that influences agricultural practices worldwide.

The environmental impacts of agriculture necessitate a nuanced understanding of the trade-offs involved in different farming practices. Intensive agriculture, while highly productive, often leads to water pollution, soil erosion, and decreased biodiversity. Sustainable agriculture practices aim to balance the needs of the present with the well-being of future generations. Techniques such as crop rotation, conservation tillage, and sustainable water management can enhance soil fertility and reduce environmental degradation. The concept of permaculture, which mimics the natural ecosystems, offers an innovative approach to sustainable land use that can rejuvenate degraded landscapes.

The role of technology in shaping the future of agriculture cannot be overstated. Precision farming, which uses GPS and IoT technologies to monitor crop health and optimize inputs, promises to make farming more efficient and environmentally friendly. Biotechnology, including genetically modified organisms (GMOs), offers the potential to increase crop yields, improve nutritional content, and reduce reliance on chemical inputs. However, these technologies also raise ethical and ecological concerns that must be carefully managed.

The study of agriculture and rural land use within the framework of AP® Human Geography equips students with the analytical tools to understand these complex issues. By examining case studies, such as the impact of soybean production in Brazil on deforestation and the role of fair trade in supporting small-scale farmers, students can appreciate the global scope of agriculture and its local impacts. Engaging with these topics encourages critical thinking about the ways in which human geography shapes and is shaped by agricultural practices, offering insights into the challenges and opportunities of creating a sustainable and equitable global food system.

As students prepare for the AP® Human Geography exam, they should focus on developing a comprehensive understanding of agricultural geography, including the factors that influence agricultural practices, the impacts of agriculture on the environment and society, and the role of innovation in addressing future challenges. This knowledge not only prepares students for academic success but also fosters a deeper appreciation for the role of agriculture in our lives and the importance of sustainable development in ensuring food security and environmental health for generations to come.

Subchapter 5.1: Agricultural Revolutions

The **First Agricultural Revolution**, also known as the Neolithic Revolution, marked a significant turning point in human history as societies transitioned from hunter-gatherer lifestyles to settled agricultural communities. This revolution, which began around 10,000 BCE, involved the domestication of plants and animals, which fundamentally changed human interaction with the environment. The ability to produce surplus food led to population growth and the development of complex societies. Key crops such as wheat, barley, and rice were domesticated in various parts of the world, laying the foundation for agricultural practices that would sustain civilizations for millennia.

Moving forward in time, the **Second Agricultural Revolution** coincided with the Industrial Revolution in the 18th and 19th centuries. This period was characterized by significant advancements in farming technology, such as the invention of the seed drill by Jethro Tull and the development of synthetic fertilizers. These innovations increased food production and efficiency, supporting rapid urbanization and industrial growth. The introduction of mechanized equipment reduced the labor required for farming, leading to significant social and economic shifts. This revolution expanded the capability of societies to support larger populations and fueled further industrialization, setting the stage for modern agricultural practices.

The **Green Revolution** of the mid-20th century represents the most recent major shift in agricultural practices. Initiated by the work of scientists like Norman Borlaug, the Green Revolution introduced high-yielding crop varieties and expanded the use of chemical fertilizers and pesticides. These innovations dramatically increased food production and are credited with preventing widespread famine in parts of the developing world. The Green Revolution also introduced irrigation techniques that made it possible to farm previously unproductive lands. However, this revolution has faced criticism for its environmental impacts, including biodiversity loss, soil degradation, and increased dependency on chemical inputs.

Each of these agricultural revolutions has played a pivotal role in shaping human societies and their relationship with the environment. The evolution of agricultural practices reflects the ongoing quest to increase food security and support growing populations. However, these advancements have also raised important questions about sustainability and the long-term health of our planet. As we look to the future, the lessons learned from past agricultural revolutions can inform the development of more sustainable farming practices that balance the need for food production with environmental conservation.

Understanding the impact of these revolutions is crucial for students preparing for the AP® Human Geography exam. Recognizing the historical context and technological advancements that led to increased agricultural productivity helps in comprehending the complex interplay between human populations and the environment. Moreover, analyzing the social, economic, and environmental consequences of these revolutions provides valuable insights into current global challenges related to food security, sustainability, and human-environment interaction.

To master this topic, students should focus on identifying the key characteristics and outcomes of each agricultural revolution. This includes understanding the technologies introduced during these periods, their effects on food production and societal development, and the environmental consequences that ensued. Engaging with a variety of resources, including academic texts, documentaries, and case studies, can deepen one's understanding of how these revolutions have shaped the world we live in today.

As we continue to face global challenges related to food security and environmental sustainability, the lessons of the past offer guidance for developing more resilient and sustainable agricultural systems. By learning from the successes and shortcomings of previous agricultural revolutions, we can work towards a future where food production is balanced with the need to preserve our planet for future generations.

Subchapter 5.2: Global Patterns of Food Production

The global patterns of food production are shaped by a myriad of factors including climate, technology, political policies, and economic practices. These patterns are critical to understand as they directly influence food security, economic stability, and environmental sustainability worldwide. Climate plays a foundational role in determining what can be grown and where. For example, the vast wheat fields of the American Midwest, the rice paddies of Asia, and the corn belts of South America are all situated in regions whose climates favor these crops. Technological advancements have also significantly altered food production landscapes. The use of genetically modified organisms (GMOs), for instance, has enabled crops to be grown in conditions that were previously unfavorable, thereby increasing food production but also sparking debates about health and environmental impacts.

Political policies and economic practices are equally influential. Subsidies for certain crops can lead to overproduction and market distortions, while trade agreements can open up or restrict access to key markets, affecting what farmers choose to grow. The European Union's Common Agricultural Policy (CAP) and the United States' Farm Bill are examples of how policy can shape agricultural landscapes and practices. Economic practices, including the shift towards monoculture and large-scale industrial farming, have increased efficiency and food production but have also raised concerns about biodiversity, soil health, and the long-term sustainability of food systems.

The environmental impacts of these global patterns are profound. Deforestation for agricultural expansion in the Amazon, water scarcity in regions heavily dependent on irrigation like California, and soil degradation in the wheat belts of Australia are just a few examples of the challenges facing global food production. These issues underscore the need for sustainable farming practices that balance food production with environmental conservation. Strategies such as crop rotation, conservation tillage, and organic farming are gaining traction as ways to mitigate some of these environmental impacts while still meeting the global demand for food.

Understanding these global patterns and their implications is essential for developing effective strategies to ensure food security, protect the environment, and support economic development. It requires a multidisciplinary approach that considers the complex interplay between climate, technology, policy, and economics. For students preparing for the AP Human Geography exam, grasping these concepts is not only crucial for academic success but also for becoming informed global citizens capable of contributing to discussions and solutions around one of humanity's most fundamental challenges: how to sustainably feed a growing world population. Engaging with case studies, such as the impact of climate change on rice production in Asia or the role of fair trade in supporting small-scale coffee farmers in Africa, can provide valuable insights into the real-world applications of these concepts. By examining these examples, students can better understand the challenges and opportunities within global food production and the importance of sustainable practices and policies in shaping the future of our food systems.

Subsistence vs. Commercial Agriculture

In the realm of agriculture, understanding the dichotomy between **subsistence** and **commercial farming** is pivotal for grasping the global patterns of food production. Subsistence agriculture is primarily about survival. It's the practice of growing food enough to feed the farmer and their family, with little to none left for trade or sale. This type of agriculture is common in parts of the world where industrialization has not fully penetrated, including regions in Africa, Asia, and Latin America. The methods and scales of production are generally traditional, relying heavily on manual labor and organic farming techniques. Subsistence farmers often utilize polyculture, growing multiple types of crops simultaneously to meet the family's dietary needs and to adapt to the challenges posed by their environment.

On the flip side, **commercial agriculture** operates on an entirely different scale and philosophy. It's characterized by large-scale operations intended to produce food and livestock for sale, both domestically and internationally. This form of agriculture leans heavily on modern technology, including advanced machinery, chemical fertilizers, pesticides, and genetically modified seeds, aiming to maximize yield and efficiency. The specialization of crops or livestock, monoculture, is a common practice in commercial farming, allowing for the mass production of a single product. This approach, while economically beneficial, raises concerns regarding sustainability, environmental degradation, and the loss of biodiversity.

The transition from subsistence to commercial agriculture is a testament to human innovation and adaptation but also brings to light the challenges of modernization. For students aiming to master AP® Human Geography, recognizing the implications of this shift is crucial. It's not just about the methods and scale of production; it's about understanding the socio-economic, environmental, and cultural impacts that these agricultural practices have on societies around the globe.

For instance, the push towards commercial agriculture has led to significant changes in rural landscapes, affecting land use patterns and leading to urbanization and rural depopulation. Moreover, the global food trade has made nations interdependent, where crop failures or surplus in one part of the world can drastically affect food prices and availability elsewhere.

Actionable steps to delve deeper into this topic include analyzing case studies that illustrate the transition from subsistence to commercial agriculture in various regions. Pay attention to the role of government policies, international aid, and global trade agreements in shaping the agricultural practices of a country. Additionally, exploring the environmental impacts, such as soil degradation, deforestation, and water scarcity, will provide a comprehensive understanding of the challenges and considerations in global food production.

Remember, the goal is not just to memorize facts but to critically analyze how agricultural practices influence and are influenced by geographical, political, and economic factors. This understanding will not only aid in scoring high on the AP® exam but also in fostering a broader perspective on the complexities of global food systems.

Subchapter 5.3: Environmental Impacts of Agriculture

The environmental impacts of agriculture are profound and multifaceted, affecting not only the natural world but also human societies on a global scale. One of the most pressing issues is **soil degradation**, a consequence of intensive farming practices that strip the land of its nutrients, leading to erosion and decreased fertility. This degradation not only reduces the land's agricultural productivity but also contributes to the loss of biodiversity as habitats are altered or destroyed. Moreover, the use of chemical fertilizers and pesticides, while boosting crop yields, can lead to water pollution, affecting freshwater resources and marine ecosystems. These chemicals can run off into rivers and seas, causing algal blooms and dead zones where aquatic life cannot survive.

Water scarcity is another significant challenge, exacerbated by agriculture's heavy reliance on irrigation. In many regions, the demand for water for crop irrigation competes with the needs of local communities and wildlife, leading to conflicts and environmental stress. Climate change compounds these issues, with changing precipitation patterns and increasing temperatures affecting crop growth, water availability, and pest distributions. To address these challenges, sustainable agricultural practices are essential. Techniques such as crop rotation, conservation tillage, and organic farming can help restore soil health and reduce dependency on chemical inputs. Integrated pest management strategies can minimize the use of harmful pesticides, while advanced irrigation technologies and water management practices can enhance water efficiency.

Agroforestry and **permaculture** are examples of holistic approaches that integrate crop production with environmental stewardship, promoting biodiversity and ecosystem resilience. These practices not only mitigate the environmental impacts of agriculture but can also improve food security and livelihoods, offering a sustainable path forward for agricultural development.

To truly grasp the environmental impacts of agriculture and the potential of sustainable practices, it is crucial to study real-world examples and current research. Investigating the effects of different agricultural systems on soil health, water quality, and biodiversity in various regions can provide valuable insights. Additionally, exploring case studies of successful sustainable agriculture projects can inspire innovative solutions and strategies for mitigating environmental impacts.

Understanding these environmental challenges and solutions is vital for anyone preparing for the AP® Human Geography exam. It requires not just memorizing facts but also connecting the dots between human activities, environmental changes, and the principles of geography. By analyzing the environmental impacts of agriculture through a geographical lens, students can develop a deeper understanding of the complex interactions between human societies and the natural world, equipping them with the knowledge and perspective needed to tackle one of the most pressing issues of our time.

Chapter 6: Industrialization and Economic Development

Industrialization marks a pivotal shift in human societies from agrarian-based economies to those dominated by industry and manufacturing. This transformation brings about significant economic development, altering not only the landscape of production but also the social and demographic fabric of nations. At the heart of industrialization is the innovation in technology, leading to increased productivity, the creation of new industries, and the urbanization of communities. As we delve into the complexities of industrialization and economic development, it's crucial to understand the role of the primary, secondary, and tertiary sectors in shaping the economic destiny of nations. The primary sector, focused on raw material extraction and agriculture, gradually gives way to the secondary sector, where manufacturing and industrial activities become the backbone of economic growth. The tertiary sector, encompassing services, then becomes increasingly significant as economies mature.

Economic sectors are not just categories of economic activity; they are stages of economic development that countries pass through as they transition from primarily agrarian societies to industrial powerhouses and finally to service-oriented economies. This evolution is accompanied by a shift in labor forces, from rural areas to cities, leading to urbanization and changes in the social structure of societies. Industrialization also introduces the concept of economic development disparities, both within and between countries. As some regions or countries industrialize more rapidly than others, disparities in wealth, living standards, and access to resources become more pronounced.

To grasp the full impact of industrialization, it's essential to explore the theories that explain why industries locate where they do. Location theory, for instance, offers insights into the factors that influence the geographical placement of industries, including access to raw materials, transportation networks, labor supply, and markets.

Understanding these theories is crucial for analyzing the economic landscapes of different regions and for predicting future trends in industrial development.

Industrialization is not without its challenges, however. Environmental degradation, the depletion of natural resources, and the displacement of communities are some of the adverse effects associated with rapid industrial growth. As we continue to explore the nuances of industrialization and economic development, it becomes clear that sustainable practices and policies are essential for mitigating these impacts. The balance between economic growth and environmental sustainability is a key focus of contemporary discussions on industrialization, highlighting the need for innovative solutions that promote both economic development and the preservation of our planet for future generations.

As students of AP® Human Geography, understanding the multifaceted nature of industrialization and economic development is fundamental. It's not just about memorizing facts and theories; it's about connecting these concepts to real-world examples and current events. Observing the ongoing industrial developments and economic shifts in various parts of the world provides valuable insights into the dynamic nature of human geography. Through this lens, we can better appreciate the complexities of our global economy and the interconnectedness of societies worldwide.

The exploration of industrial location theories further deepens our understanding of economic geography. Alfred Weber's Least Cost Theory, for instance, highlights the importance of minimizing costs to maximize profits, influencing decisions on the placement of industries. This theory, along with others like the Central Place Theory and Hotelling's Model, provides a framework for understanding the spatial organization of economies. These theories are not only academic concepts but also practical tools used by businesses and governments to make informed decisions about where to invest and develop infrastructure. By analyzing case studies that apply these theories, students can see the practical implications of geographical decisions in the real world.

Moreover, the transition from industrialization to a service-oriented economy marks a significant shift in the economic landscape. The rise of the tertiary and quaternary sectors reflects changes in consumer behavior, technological advancements, and the globalization of markets. This shift has profound implications for employment patterns, urban development, and international trade. The knowledge economy, characterized by the importance of information technology and service industries, underscores the need for a skilled workforce and innovative thinking in the modern world.

Globalization, another key aspect of economic development, has transformed the way countries interact and compete on the international stage. It has led to increased economic interdependence among nations, but also to greater competition for jobs, resources, and markets. Understanding the effects of globalization, including the spread of multinational corporations and the outsourcing of jobs, is crucial for grasitating the current economic climate. The role of international organizations, such as the World Trade Organization (WTO) and the International Monetary Fund (IMF), in shaping economic policies and practices globally, also warrants attention.

The disparities in economic development between and within countries pose significant challenges. Issues such as income inequality, access to education and healthcare, and sustainable development are at the forefront of international discussions. Addressing these disparities requires a multifaceted approach, including investment in education, infrastructure, and technology, as well as policies that promote fair trade and environmental protection.

For students preparing for the AP® Human Geography exam, mastering the concepts of industrialization and economic development involves not only understanding the theories and models that explain economic activities and patterns but also being able to apply this knowledge to analyze current events and global trends. Engaging with real-world examples, from the deindustrialization of traditional manufacturing hubs to the rise of tech cities and the challenges of sustainable development, brings these concepts to life.

By examining the environmental impacts of industrial activities and exploring sustainable practices, students can develop a nuanced perspective on economic development. This includes studying the principles of green technology, renewable energy sources, and sustainable urban planning. The goal is to envision a future where economic growth does not come at the expense of the environment or social equity.

In preparing for the exam, students should focus on developing critical thinking and analytical skills. This involves not just memorizing facts but also being able to interpret maps, data, and case studies; evaluate different viewpoints; and construct well-reasoned arguments. Practice questions, especially those that simulate the format of the AP® exam, can help students apply their knowledge and improve their test-taking strategies.

Ultimately, the study of industrialization and economic development in AP® Human Geography equips students with a deeper understanding of the world around them. It encourages them to think critically about the challenges and opportunities of our global economy and to consider their role in shaping a more equitable and sustainable future. Through diligent study and engagement with the material, students can build the foundation necessary to excel on the AP® exam and beyond, in their academic and professional pursuits.

Subchapter 6.1: Economic Sectors (Primary, Secondary, Tertiary)

The economic sectors, categorized into **primary**, **secondary**, and **tertiary**, represent the stages through which a country's economy evolves from basic to more complex forms of activity. Each of these sectors plays a pivotal role in shaping the economic landscape, influencing everything from employment patterns to GDP growth. Understanding these sectors is crucial for grasping the broader concepts of industrialization and economic development, especially in the context of the AP® Human Geography exam.

Primary Sector: This sector is the backbone of any economy, focusing on the extraction of raw materials directly from the Earth. Activities include agriculture, mining, forestry, and fishing. Despite its fundamental role, the primary sector often employs a smaller percentage of the workforce in developed countries due to technological advancements and efficiency improvements. However, in developing nations, a large portion of the population may still be engaged in primary activities, reflecting a different stage of economic development.

Secondary Sector: Marked by the transformation of raw materials into finished goods, the secondary sector encompasses all forms of manufacturing and construction. This sector is critical for a country's industrial growth, as it signifies a move towards more value-added activities. The rise of the secondary sector is often associated with the period of industrialization, where technological innovation leads to mass production and diversification of the economy. Countries in the midst of rapid industrialization will typically see a boom in secondary sector activities.

Tertiary Sector: The service sector, or tertiary sector, includes activities where services are provided to businesses and consumers. This can range from banking and education to healthcare and entertainment. In advanced economies, the tertiary sector dominates, employing the majority of the workforce and contributing significantly to GDP. The growth of the tertiary sector reflects a shift towards an information-based economy, where knowledge and services become the primary drivers of economic activity.

To excel in the AP® Human Geography exam, students should not only memorize these definitions but also understand the implications of the shift from primary through secondary to tertiary sectors. This transition often mirrors a country's development path, from a focus on agriculture to industrialization, and finally to a service-oriented economy.

Actionable Steps for Students:
1. **Case Studies**: Examine various countries at different stages of economic development. Identify which sector is predominant and discuss the socio-economic implications of this predominance.
2. **Data Analysis**: Look at the employment and GDP contribution of each sector within a country over time. This can reveal trends in economic development and shifts in the focus of economic activity.
3. **Comparative Studies**: Compare and contrast the economic structures of developed and developing countries. Pay attention to how the balance between the sectors differs and the factors driving these differences.

By delving into these areas, students can develop a nuanced understanding of how economic sectors influence the geography of industrialization and economic development. This knowledge not only prepares students for the AP® Human Geography exam but also equips them with insights into the complexities of the global economy. Engaging with real-world examples and current data will make these concepts more relatable and easier to grasp, fostering a deeper appreciation for the subject matter.

Subchapter 6.2: Industrial Location Theories

Alfred Weber's Least Cost Theory is a cornerstone of industrial location theories, positing that industries are located to minimize three critical costs: transportation, labor, and agglomeration. This theory suggests that an optimal location is found at a point where these costs are at their lowest. For instance, industries requiring heavy raw materials might be situated near the source of these materials to reduce transportation costs. Similarly, industries might be located in areas with lower labor costs to minimize expenses, although this can be balanced against the need for skilled labor which might be more expensive but necessary for the industry's success.

Another significant theory is the Central Place Theory, developed by Walter Christaller, which explains how and where central places in the urban hierarchy (e.g., small towns, cities) should be functionally and spatially distributed to serve as trading centers for the surrounding area. This theory is based on the assumption that settlements simply function to provide goods and services to their surrounding catchment area and that there are thresholds of demand required to support the presence of various services.

Hotelling's Model, or the theory of locational interdependence, suggests that industries choose locations based on the locations of their competitors. This theory is particularly relevant in the retail sector where businesses might cluster in the same area to benefit from the existing customer base, despite the increased competition that comes with proximity. This clustering can be seen in the way fast-food restaurants often locate near each other in busy shopping districts.

The concept of agglomeration economies plays a crucial role in industrial location decisions. Agglomeration economies refer to the benefits that companies obtain by locating close to each other. These benefits include shared suppliers, access to specialized labor, and the facilitation of idea sharing and innovation. Silicon Valley in California exemplifies the power of agglomeration economies, where the concentration of high-tech companies has spurred innovation, attracted skilled labor, and drawn investment.

Actionable Steps for Students:

1. **Identify Examples**: Look for real-world examples of each theory in action. For instance, research why certain manufacturing industries are concentrated in specific regions of the United States or globally.

2. **Map Analysis**: Use maps to identify patterns of industrial locations and consider the factors that might have influenced these patterns. This could involve looking at the distribution of tech companies in Silicon Valley or automotive manufacturers in the Midwest.

3. **Case Studies**: Dive into case studies that explore the relocation of industries. For example, study why a company might move its manufacturing from one country to another and how this relates to the theories discussed.

4. **Debate and Discussion**: Engage in debates or discussions about the relevance of these theories today, especially in the context of globalization and technological advancements. Consider how the rise of remote work and digital technology might impact traditional theories of industrial location.

Understanding these theories and their applications provides a framework for analyzing economic landscapes and predicting future trends in industrial development. It's not just about where industries are now but understanding the underlying principles that dictate these locations. This knowledge is crucial for anyone looking to excel in AP® Human Geography, providing the tools needed to analyze and interpret the economic activities and patterns that shape our world.

Weber's Least Cost Theory

Alfred Weber's Least Cost Theory, developed in the early 20th century, remains a vital concept for understanding the strategic considerations behind the geographical placement of industries. This theory intricately connects to the broader themes of industrialization and economic development by emphasizing the importance of minimizing production costs to enhance profitability. At its core, Weber's theory identifies three primary cost factors that influence industrial location decisions: transportation, labor, and agglomeration.

Transportation costs often dictate the movement and location of industries, as businesses strive to position themselves in a manner that reduces the expense of moving raw materials to the production site and finished goods to the market. This aspect of the theory underscores the significance of logistical planning and infrastructure in industrial geography, highlighting the need for efficient transportation networks. For students aiming to master AP® Human Geography, understanding the impact of transportation on industrial location offers insights into the spatial patterns of economic activities and their environmental implications.

Labor costs also play a crucial role in determining where industries choose to establish operations. Industries may gravitate towards regions where labor is cheaper, yet they must balance this with the need for a skilled workforce. This component of Weber's theory illustrates the complex interplay between economic considerations and social factors, such as education and workforce development. It prompts a deeper exploration of how industrial locations can influence and be influenced by demographic trends, migration patterns, and social policies.

Agglomeration, the third critical factor, refers to the benefits that companies gain by locating near each other. This phenomenon can lead to the development of industrial clusters, where businesses enjoy shared services, access to specialized suppliers, and a pool of skilled labor. The concept of agglomeration economies is particularly relevant in today's globalized economy, where innovation and collaboration are key drivers of industrial competitiveness. By studying examples of agglomeration, such as tech hubs and manufacturing districts, students can gain insights into the dynamics of economic geography and the factors that contribute to regional economic growth.

Actionable Steps for Students:

- **Examine Historical and Contemporary Examples**: Investigate how Weber's Least Cost Theory has influenced the location of various industries over time, from the steel mills of the past to the tech startups of today. Analyzing these examples will help students understand the theory's application and relevance in different historical and economic contexts.

- **Geographical Analysis**: Use maps and spatial data to explore the distribution of industries within a particular region or country. Identify patterns that reflect the principles of Weber's theory, such as the concentration of manufacturing plants near raw material sources or major transportation hubs.

- **Case Study Research**: Delve into case studies of companies that have relocated their manufacturing or service facilities. Explore the reasons behind these decisions and how they align with the cost-minimization strategies outlined by Weber. This research can provide practical examples of the theory in action, illustrating its impact on real-world economic and geographical landscapes.

By engaging with Weber's Least Cost Theory through these actionable steps, students can develop a nuanced understanding of industrial location decisions and their broader implications for economic development and environmental sustainability. This exploration will equip students with the analytical tools needed to dissect complex geographical phenomena, preparing them for success on the AP® Human Geography exam and beyond. As they navigate the intricacies of economic geography, students will discover the interconnectedness of human activities and the physical environment, fostering a comprehensive perspective on the challenges and opportunities facing our global society.

Subchapter 6.3: Globalization and Economic Disparities

Globalization has significantly influenced economic development across the globe, leading to disparities that are evident in various dimensions such as income, access to healthcare, education, and technology. These disparities are not just between countries but also within them, affecting rural and urban areas differently. To understand the impact of globalization on economic development disparities, it's essential to delve into the mechanisms through which globalization operates – including trade liberalization, foreign direct investment (FDI), technological transfer, and the role of international financial institutions like the World Trade Organization (WTO) and the International Monetary Fund (IMF).

Trade liberalization has allowed countries to specialize in the production of goods and services in which they have a comparative advantage, leading to efficiency gains and economic growth. However, this has also resulted in job losses in sectors that are not competitive internationally, often without adequate social safety nets to support affected workers. Similarly, while FDI can bring capital, technology, and management expertise to host countries, it can also lead to environmental degradation and exploitation of labor if not properly regulated.

Technological transfer through globalization has been a double-edged sword. On one hand, it has enabled leapfrogging in developing countries, allowing them to adopt advanced technologies without going through intermediary stages. On the other hand, it has also widened the digital divide, as countries with the infrastructure and skills to leverage these technologies have benefited more than those without.

The role of international financial institutions in shaping economic policies in developing countries has been controversial. While they provide necessary financial resources, their structural adjustment programs have often been criticized for prioritizing fiscal austerity and market liberalization over social spending, leading to increased poverty and inequality in some cases.

To address these disparities, a multifaceted approach is necessary. Policies aimed at enhancing the competitiveness of domestic industries, investing in education and skills development, and creating social safety nets can help mitigate the adverse effects of globalization. Additionally, international cooperation is crucial to ensure that globalization leads to a more equitable distribution of its benefits. This includes reforming global financial governance structures to give developing countries a greater voice, as well as implementing international agreements that protect labor rights and the environment.

Understanding the nuances of globalization's impact on economic development disparities is crucial for students preparing for the AP Human Geography exam. It not only helps in grasping the complex interplay between global economic forces and local realities but also in envisioning solutions that can lead to more inclusive and sustainable development outcomes.

Case Studies of Newly Industrialized Countries

The transformation of Newly Industrialized Countries (NICs) offers a compelling narrative of economic development and the nuanced impacts of globalization. These countries, having transitioned from primarily agricultural economies to more industrialized and diversified economic structures, present valuable lessons in managing globalization's opportunities and challenges. South Korea, Singapore, Taiwan, and Brazil exemplify the varied pathways through which NICs have navigated the complexities of global economic integration, each leveraging unique strategies to foster economic growth, technological advancement, and social development.

South Korea's journey from a war-torn nation to a leading global technology hub underscores the critical role of government policy in directing economic development. By prioritizing education, fostering a strong work ethic, and implementing strategic economic plans, South Korea cultivated a competitive edge in electronics, automobiles, and shipbuilding. This case illustrates the importance of cohesive national strategies that align education, industrial policy, and international trade to achieve rapid industrialization.

Singapore's story highlights the significance of strategic location and investment in human capital. By establishing itself as a global financial center and a hub for trade and logistics, Singapore demonstrates how effective governance and an outward-oriented economic strategy can transform a small island with limited natural resources into a thriving economy. This case emphasizes the value of creating a conducive environment for investment, innovation, and talent development.

Taiwan's economic ascent, driven by the development of high-tech industries and a robust small and medium-sized enterprise (SME) sector, showcases the power of innovation and entrepreneurship. Taiwan's emphasis on research and development, coupled with its ability to adapt to global market trends, has positioned it as a leader in semiconductors and information technology. This narrative underscores the role of innovation ecosystems and the need to support SMEs as engines of growth and employment.

Brazil's experience reflects the complexities of economic development in a resource-rich country. Despite its significant agricultural, mineral, and energy resources, Brazil has faced challenges in translating these assets into sustainable economic development. The Brazilian case points to the necessity of diversifying the economy, investing in infrastructure, and addressing social inequalities to harness globalization's full potential.

These case studies of NICs reveal several key strategies for mastering AP Human Geography concepts related to industrialization and economic development. First, the importance of government policy and planning in guiding economic transformation cannot be overstated. Effective policies that support education, innovation, and infrastructure development are crucial. Second, the role of globalization in providing opportunities for growth through trade, investment, and technological transfer is evident across all NICs. However, managing the adverse effects of globalization, such as environmental degradation and social inequality, remains a significant challenge. Third, the cases highlight the need for economic diversification and the development of competitive industries to sustain growth and reduce vulnerability to global market fluctuations.

For students aiming to excel in the AP Human Geography exam, understanding the dynamics of NICs offers valuable insights into the processes of economic development and the multifaceted impacts of globalization. Analyzing these case studies provides a practical context for applying geographic concepts and theories, enhancing the ability to think critically about the factors that influence economic development and the spatial variations in industrialization and economic growth.

Chapter 7: Urbanization and Cities

Urbanization and cities represent a fundamental shift in human geography, marking the transition from rural to urban living. This transformation is driven by various factors, including the search for employment, access to services, and the allure of urban life. Urbanization is not merely a change in physical space but also brings about significant socio-economic and environmental changes. The process of urbanization often leads to the expansion of cities into surrounding rural areas, a phenomenon known as urban sprawl. This sprawl can have various implications, from altering land use patterns to increasing the demand for infrastructure and services. As cities expand, they often absorb nearby towns and villages, integrating them into the urban fabric. This integration can lead to a diverse range of urban forms, from densely packed city centers to sprawling suburbs.

One of the critical aspects of urbanization is the development of urban models, which help geographers and urban planners understand and predict the growth patterns of cities. Models such as the Burgess concentric zone model, the Hoyt sector model, and the Harris and Ullman multiple nuclei model offer insights into how cities develop and expand. These models suggest that urban growth is not random but follows certain patterns influenced by factors such as economic activities, topography, and transportation networks. For instance, the concentric zone model proposes that cities grow outward in rings from a central business district, while the sector model suggests that cities expand in wedges or sectors along transportation routes.

Another significant aspect of urbanization is suburbanization, which refers to the movement of populations from city centers to the suburbs. This trend is driven by various factors, including the desire for more spacious and affordable housing, better schools, and a perceived higher quality of life. However, suburbanization also comes with challenges, such as increased reliance on automobiles, leading to traffic congestion and higher greenhouse gas emissions. Additionally, the movement to the suburbs can contribute to socio-economic segregation, with wealthier populations moving away from city centers, leaving behind lower-income residents who may have less access to services and opportunities.

Urban sprawl and suburbanization raise important questions about sustainability and the future of urban living. As cities continue to grow, they face challenges related to transportation, housing, environmental sustainability, and social equity. Addressing these challenges requires innovative urban planning and policy solutions that promote more compact, efficient, and inclusive urban development. Strategies such as smart growth, which focuses on creating walkable communities with a mix of housing and commercial spaces, and green urbanism, which emphasizes the integration of green spaces and sustainable infrastructure, are increasingly being explored as ways to make cities more livable and sustainable.

The study of urbanization and cities in AP Human Geography provides students with a framework to understand the complex dynamics of urban growth and development. By examining different urban models, trends in urbanization and suburbanization, and the challenges and opportunities associated with urban living, students can gain insights into how geographic concepts shape the world around us. As we continue to witness rapid urbanization globally, the importance of sustainable urban planning and development becomes ever more critical.

Urban planning and sustainability are pivotal in addressing the challenges posed by urban sprawl and suburbanization. Effective urban planning can lead to the development of cities that are not only more sustainable but also more equitable and livable. This involves the adoption of mixed-use development, where residential, commercial, and recreational spaces coexist, reducing the need for long commutes and promoting a more community-oriented lifestyle. Furthermore, the integration of public transportation systems can significantly reduce reliance on personal vehicles, decrease traffic congestion, and lower carbon emissions, contributing to a healthier urban environment.

The concept of green urbanism takes this a step further by incorporating environmental principles into urban design. This includes the preservation of natural spaces within urban areas, the promotion of renewable energy sources, and the implementation of green building practices. Such initiatives not only enhance the quality of life for urban residents but also help cities adapt to the challenges of climate change by reducing their environmental footprint.

In addition to physical planning and design, social equity is a critical component of sustainable urban development. Ensuring access to affordable housing, quality education, and healthcare for all residents helps to mitigate the socio-economic divides that can be exacerbated by urbanization. Community engagement and participatory planning processes are essential in creating urban spaces that reflect the needs and desires of their diverse populations.

The role of technology in urban planning cannot be overlooked. Geographic Information Systems (GIS) and other digital tools enable urban planners to analyze spatial data, model urban growth scenarios, and engage with the public in more interactive and meaningful ways. These technologies can help in making informed decisions that promote sustainable urban development.

For students of AP Human Geography, understanding the principles of urban planning and sustainability is crucial. It provides a lens through which to view the challenges and opportunities of urbanization in a global context. By exploring case studies of cities that have successfully implemented sustainable urban development strategies, students can appreciate the potential for positive change in urban environments.

Moreover, the examination of urbanization and its impacts prepares students for the AP Human Geography exam by equipping them with the analytical tools needed to critically assess urban phenomena. They learn to apply geographic concepts to real-world situations, enhancing their ability to think spatially and understand the interconnectedness of human and environmental systems.

As urban areas continue to evolve, the importance of sustainable development practices becomes increasingly evident. By fostering an understanding of these practices among young learners, we can inspire a new generation of thinkers and planners committed to creating more sustainable, equitable, and livable urban futures. Through the study of urbanization and cities, students are not only preparing for academic success but are also gaining the knowledge and skills necessary to contribute to the well-being of urban societies around the globe.

Subchapter 7.1: Urban Models (Burgess, Hoyt, Harris-Ullman)

The Burgess concentric zone model, the Hoyt sector model, and the Harris-Ullman multiple nuclei model each offer unique perspectives on urban development and structure. The Burgess model conceptualizes the city as a series of concentric circles, with the central business district (CBD) at its core, surrounded by zones of transition, working-class homes, better residences, and commuters' zone. This model highlights the importance of economic activities in shaping the urban landscape, suggesting that cities expand outward from the center, with newer developments pushing older ones to the periphery. The Hoyt sector model, on the other hand, proposes that cities grow in sectors rather than rings. According to this model, the city is organized into wedges or sectors that extend outward from the CBD, with different sectors for industry, low-income housing, and high-income housing. This model emphasizes the role of transportation routes in guiding urban expansion, with high-income residential areas typically situated along desirable environmental features or away from industrial zones. The Harris and Ullman multiple nuclei model diverges from the notion of a single center and instead suggests that cities have multiple centers or nuclei around which different types of activities cluster. These nuclei form as a result of specific historical, economic, or environmental factors, leading to a city that is a complex patchwork of specialized zones. This model reflects the reality of many modern cities, where distinct districts, such as governmental, financial, and industrial areas, develop independently of each other.

Understanding these models is crucial for grasping the dynamics of urban growth and the spatial distribution of different urban functions. Each model offers insights into the factors that influence urban form, from economic activities and transportation networks to historical developments and environmental constraints. However, it's important to recognize that no single model can fully capture the complexity of urban development. Cities often exhibit characteristics of all three models, with their unique historical contexts and geographical settings shaping their growth patterns. For students preparing for the AP Human Geography exam, being able to compare and contrast these models, and understanding their applicability to real-world cities, is essential. This knowledge not only aids in mastering the exam content but also in developing a nuanced understanding of urban geography.

Practical application of these models in analyzing urban areas can enhance your analytical skills. For instance, examining a city's layout and identifying areas that correspond to the different zones in the Burgess model, or sectors in the Hoyt model, can provide insights into the city's development history and its socio-economic structure. Similarly, identifying multiple nuclei in a city can reveal how economic, cultural, or environmental factors have influenced its growth. This analytical approach can be particularly useful in answering free-response questions (FRQs) on the AP exam, where you may be asked to analyze urban patterns and processes.

To effectively prepare for the AP Human Geography exam, it's beneficial to engage with these models actively. This can involve mapping exercises, where you apply each model to analyze the structure of different cities, or case studies, where you examine how a city's development aligns with or diverges from the predicted patterns. Additionally, discussing these models in study groups can deepen your understanding, as you'll be exposed to diverse perspectives and interpretations. Remember, the goal is not just to memorize the models but to understand their underlying principles and how they can be used to interpret the complex realities of urban geography.

In summary, mastering the concepts of the Burgess, Hoyt, and Harris-Ullman models is a stepping stone towards excelling in the urbanization and cities portion of the AP Human Geography exam. By understanding these models, you'll be better equipped to analyze urban patterns and processes, which is a critical skill not only for the exam but also for understanding the broader dynamics of human geography.

Subchapter 7.2: Suburbanization and Urban Sprawl

Suburbanization and urban sprawl are phenomena that have reshaped the landscape of American cities and their outskirts, reflecting broader socio-economic trends and individual preferences for living spaces. Suburbanization, the migration of people from urban centers to the suburbs, has been driven by a quest for more spacious and affordable housing, better schools, and a perceived higher quality of life outside the congested city centers. This movement has been facilitated by advancements in transportation and infrastructure, allowing people to commute more easily to urban jobs from their suburban homes. However, this shift has also led to urban sprawl, a pattern of uncontrolled expansion of urban areas into the surrounding rural land. The consequences of urban sprawl include increased traffic congestion, loss of agricultural land and open spaces, and a rise in pollution due to greater dependency on automobiles.

Urban sprawl has significant implications for environmental sustainability and resource consumption. As cities expand outward, the infrastructure needs grow exponentially, including roads, utilities, and services, which often leads to inefficient use of resources and increased environmental degradation. The spread of low-density development makes public transportation less viable, leading to increased car dependency, higher greenhouse gas emissions, and worsening air quality. Additionally, the loss of green spaces and habitats can have profound effects on biodiversity and ecosystem services.

To combat the negative impacts of suburbanization and urban sprawl, several strategies can be employed. Smart growth initiatives aim to concentrate growth in compact, walkable urban areas to reduce sprawl, preserve open space, and promote sustainable living. These strategies include developing mixed-use spaces where residential, commercial, and recreational facilities are integrated, encouraging the use of public transportation, and preserving green belts and agricultural land around urban areas. Zoning laws and urban growth boundaries can also be effective tools in controlling sprawl, by limiting the extent of urban development and encouraging higher-density housing in existing urban areas.

Infill development is another approach to mitigate the effects of sprawl, focusing on redeveloping vacant or underused parcels within urban areas, rather than expanding into new land. This can help revitalize cities, make efficient use of infrastructure, and reduce the pressure on undeveloped land. Additionally, policies promoting affordable housing in urban centers can help counteract the socio-economic segregation often seen in suburbanization trends, by providing more equitable access to resources and opportunities for all residents.

Public transportation plays a crucial role in sustainable urban development. Investing in efficient and accessible public transit systems can reduce the reliance on personal vehicles, decrease traffic congestion, and lower carbon emissions. Encouraging biking and walking through the development of bike lanes and pedestrian-friendly streetscapes can also contribute to more sustainable urban environments.

For students preparing for the AP Human Geography exam, understanding the dynamics of suburbanization and urban sprawl is essential. It involves recognizing the causes and consequences of these trends, as well as evaluating the effectiveness of different strategies to address them. This knowledge not only aids in mastering the exam content but also in developing a nuanced understanding of the challenges and opportunities in urban development. Engaging with these topics encourages critical thinking about how geographic concepts apply to real-world issues, fostering a deeper appreciation for the complexities of human-environment interactions.

Case studies of cities that have successfully implemented smart growth policies or other anti-sprawl measures can provide valuable insights into practical solutions. Examining the experiences of cities like Portland, Oregon, with its urban growth boundary, or the redevelopment projects in cities like Baltimore, Maryland, can offer examples of how urban planning and policy can shape more sustainable and livable urban futures. These case studies not only enrich students' understanding of the material but also equip them with examples that can be used in exam responses to demonstrate a comprehensive grasp of the subject matter.

By exploring the multifaceted issues of suburbanization and urban sprawl, students can better understand the interplay between human choices, policy decisions, and environmental consequences. This understanding is crucial for envisioning and advocating for more sustainable and equitable urban development practices in the future.

Subchapter 7.3: Urban Planning and Sustainability

Urban planning and sustainability are intertwined concepts that address the environmental, economic, and social challenges of urban sprawl and suburbanization. The goal is to create urban areas that are livable, resilient, and equitable. **Sustainable urban planning** focuses on minimizing the ecological footprint of cities while enhancing the quality of life for all residents. This involves a variety of strategies, such as **green infrastructure, energy efficiency**, and **sustainable transportation systems**. Green infrastructure includes parks, green roofs, and urban forests that provide essential ecosystem services, reduce heat island effects, and improve air quality. Energy efficiency can be enhanced through the design of buildings and the use of renewable energy sources, reducing the overall energy consumption of the city. Sustainable transportation systems, including public transit, biking, and walking paths, reduce reliance on fossil fuels and promote healthier lifestyles.

Community involvement is crucial in sustainable urban planning. Engaging local communities in the planning process ensures that the needs and desires of residents are met, fostering a sense of ownership and responsibility towards the urban environment. This participatory approach can lead to more innovative solutions and stronger support for sustainability initiatives. **Zoning laws** and **urban policies** also play a significant role in shaping sustainable cities. By regulating land use, these laws can promote higher density development, preserve open spaces, and encourage mixed-use developments that reduce the need for long commutes.

Resilience planning is another critical aspect of sustainable urban development. Cities must be designed to withstand natural disasters, climate change impacts, and other shocks. This includes creating robust infrastructure, protecting natural buffers such as wetlands, and developing emergency response strategies. By prioritizing resilience, cities can protect their residents and assets, reducing the costs and impacts of future disasters.

Affordable housing is a key component of social sustainability in urban planning. Ensuring access to safe, affordable housing for all residents helps to reduce inequality and prevent the displacement of low-income communities. This can be achieved through a variety of mechanisms, including inclusionary zoning, housing subsidies, and the development of social housing projects.

Sustainable urban planning is not only about addressing current challenges but also about anticipating future needs. This requires a forward-thinking approach that considers long-term environmental sustainability, economic viability, and social equity. By integrating these principles into urban planning, cities can become more sustainable, resilient, and livable places for current and future generations.

For students preparing for the AP Human Geography exam, understanding the principles and practices of sustainable urban planning is essential. This knowledge will not only help them excel in the exam but also equip them with the insights needed to contribute to the development of sustainable urban areas in their future careers. Engaging with real-world examples of sustainable urban planning initiatives can provide valuable context and deepen students' understanding of the subject. Whether it's analyzing the success of a green infrastructure project in a nearby city or evaluating the impact of zoning laws on urban development patterns, practical examples can bring the concepts of urban planning and sustainability to life. By exploring these topics, students can develop a comprehensive understanding of how geographic concepts apply to the challenges and opportunities of urbanization, preparing them for success on the AP Human Geography exam and beyond.

Chapter 8: Human-Environment Interaction

Environmental sustainability is a crucial aspect of human-environment interaction, focusing on how societies can meet the needs of the present without compromising the ability of future generations to meet their own needs. This involves a careful balance of resource use, development strategies, and the incorporation of renewable energy sources to minimize environmental degradation and promote a healthy ecosystem. As we delve into the intricacies of environmental sustainability, it becomes evident that this is not just an environmental imperative but also a socio-economic challenge that requires innovative solutions and collaborative efforts across global, national, and local levels.

One of the key components of environmental sustainability is the conservation of natural resources. This includes strategies to reduce water usage, enhance energy efficiency, and promote sustainable land use practices. By adopting methods such as rainwater harvesting, solar energy installations, and sustainable agriculture practices, communities can significantly reduce their environmental footprint. These practices not only contribute to the conservation of the environment but also offer economic benefits by reducing costs and creating green jobs.

Another vital aspect is the reduction of pollution and waste. Through the implementation of recycling programs, waste-to-energy initiatives, and pollution control measures, societies can mitigate the harmful effects of waste accumulation and environmental contaminants. These efforts are essential for protecting air and water quality, preserving biodiversity, and ensuring the health and well-being of all living organisms.

The concept of sustainable development also emphasizes the importance of social equity and inclusivity in environmental decision-making. This means ensuring that all members of society have access to clean air, water, and land, and are involved in the processes that affect their environment. It challenges us to rethink our development patterns and strive for a more equitable distribution of resources and opportunities.

As we explore the multifaceted relationship between humans and their environment, it becomes clear that achieving environmental sustainability is a complex but achievable goal. It requires a comprehensive understanding of ecological principles, innovative thinking, and a commitment to action from individuals, communities, and governments alike. Through education, policy reform, and community engagement, we can work towards a more sustainable and equitable future for all.

Adapting to climate change is another critical dimension of human-environment interaction, highlighting the need for societies to develop resilience against the increasing frequency and intensity of extreme weather events. Strategies such as building flood defenses, creating drought-resistant crops, and designing cities that can withstand extreme temperatures are becoming increasingly important. These measures not only safeguard communities but also protect economies from the devastating impacts of climate change. By integrating climate adaptation into planning and development processes, we can ensure that our social and economic systems remain robust in the face of environmental uncertainties.

In addition to adaptation, there is a growing emphasis on mitigation efforts to reduce the causes of climate change. This involves reducing greenhouse gas emissions through cleaner energy sources, enhancing carbon sinks, and promoting sustainable transportation options. Transitioning to a low-carbon economy requires innovation and investment in green technologies, as well as a shift in consumer behavior towards more sustainable practices. By taking proactive steps to mitigate climate change, we can limit global warming and its associated risks.

Engagement and collaboration among stakeholders at all levels are essential for advancing environmental sustainability. This includes partnerships between governments, businesses, non-profit organizations, and communities. Such collaborations can lead to the development and implementation of policies and practices that support sustainable development goals. Public participation in environmental decision-making ensures that diverse perspectives are considered, leading to more effective and equitable solutions.

Education plays a pivotal role in fostering a culture of sustainability. By incorporating environmental education into school curricula and community programs, we can raise awareness about the importance of sustainability and empower individuals with the knowledge and skills needed to make informed decisions. Educating the next generation about the challenges and opportunities of environmental sustainability is crucial for ensuring long-term success in our efforts to protect the planet.

In conclusion, the journey towards environmental sustainability is a collective endeavor that requires a multifaceted approach. From conserving natural resources and reducing pollution to adapting to climate change and promoting social equity, each aspect of sustainability is interconnected. By embracing innovative solutions, fostering collaboration, and prioritizing education, we can navigate the complexities of human-environment interaction and work towards a sustainable and prosperous future for all.

Subchapter 8.1: Environmental Sustainability

Environmental sustainability requires a multifaceted approach, integrating both local and global perspectives to address the pressing environmental issues of our time. One of the foundational steps towards achieving this goal is the promotion of renewable energy sources. Transitioning from fossil fuels to solar, wind, and hydroelectric power can significantly reduce carbon emissions, a major contributor to global warming. Communities and nations alike must invest in these technologies, providing incentives for their adoption and creating infrastructure that supports their widespread use.

Another critical strategy is the implementation of sustainable agriculture practices. Traditional farming methods often lead to soil degradation, water scarcity, and biodiversity loss. By adopting practices such as crop rotation, permaculture, and organic farming, we can produce food in a way that sustains the earth's resources rather than depleting them. This not only ensures food security for future generations but also reduces the environmental impact of agriculture.

Water conservation is equally important in the quest for environmental sustainability. Innovative water management techniques, including rainwater harvesting, drip irrigation, and wastewater treatment, can help conserve this precious resource. Public awareness campaigns and educational programs are essential in promoting water-saving practices among individuals and communities.

Waste reduction is another key area of focus. Reducing, reusing, and recycling can significantly lower the amount of waste sent to landfills and decrease greenhouse gas emissions. Governments and organizations should encourage the development of products that are designed to have a longer life, be repairable, or be fully recyclable. Community-based initiatives, such as composting programs and zero-waste campaigns, can also play a vital role in minimizing waste.

Biodiversity conservation efforts are crucial for maintaining the balance of ecosystems. Protecting natural habitats, restoring degraded areas, and implementing policies that prevent overexploitation of species are necessary steps to preserve the planet's biodiversity. Public and private sectors must collaborate to create and enforce regulations that protect endangered species and their habitats.

Public transportation and sustainable urban planning can greatly reduce the carbon footprint of cities. Developing efficient public transit systems, promoting cycling and walking, and designing cities to be more compact and walkable can decrease reliance on personal vehicles and reduce air pollution. Green spaces and urban parks not only contribute to the aesthetic and recreational value of cities but also play a role in cooling urban areas and supporting local wildlife.

Involving local communities in environmental conservation efforts is essential for their success. Community-led initiatives, such as tree planting, clean-up drives, and conservation projects, empower individuals to take action and make a positive impact on their environment. Education and outreach programs can raise awareness about the importance of sustainability and inspire collective action towards a more sustainable future.

By adopting these strategies, we can work towards a world where economic development and environmental conservation go hand in hand. It is through the collective efforts of individuals, communities, governments, and businesses that we can achieve the goal of environmental sustainability. Engaging in sustainable practices not only benefits the planet but also enhances the quality of life for all its inhabitants.

Subchapter 8.2: Climate Change and Human Geography

Climate change significantly alters the dynamics of human geography by impacting where and how people can live, affecting migration patterns, and reshaping economic activities. As temperatures rise, sea levels elevate, and weather patterns become more unpredictable, communities, especially those in vulnerable areas, are forced to adapt to new environmental realities. This adaptation often involves relocating to areas less susceptible to climate change effects, a phenomenon increasingly observed as "climate migration." Coastal cities face the threat of inundation, prompting urban planners to rethink city designs to incorporate flood defenses and water management systems that can handle rising sea levels. Similarly, agricultural zones shift due to changing rainfall patterns and temperatures, necessitating adjustments in crop selection and farming practices to ensure food security. These shifts not only affect local economies but also have the potential to alter global trade patterns as regions traditionally dependent on certain crops become less viable.

Moreover, climate change exacerbates existing social inequalities, hitting hardest those communities least equipped to adapt. Low-income populations, often residing in areas more prone to flooding, drought, and other climate-related challenges, find themselves at a disproportionate risk. Addressing these disparities requires targeted policies that not only focus on mitigating climate change effects but also on enhancing the resilience of vulnerable communities. This includes investing in sustainable infrastructure, providing access to education and resources needed for adaptation, and ensuring that all segments of society are represented in climate adaptation planning processes.

The role of technology in adapting to climate change is increasingly critical. Geographic Information Systems (GIS) and remote sensing technologies offer valuable tools for monitoring climate change impacts and planning for adaptation. These technologies can help identify areas at risk of sea-level rise, predict agricultural shifts, and model urban expansion patterns that consider future climate scenarios. By leveraging data-driven insights, policymakers, urban planners, and communities can make informed decisions that minimize climate change risks and capitalize on new opportunities presented by these shifts.

Education and community engagement are pivotal in fostering a culture of sustainability and resilience. By raising awareness about the impacts of climate change on human geography, individuals can be empowered to take action, whether through advocating for sustainable practices, participating in local planning processes, or adopting lifestyle changes that reduce their carbon footprint. Schools and educational institutions play a crucial role in this process, integrating climate education into curricula to prepare future generations for the challenges and opportunities ahead.

In the face of climate change, the interconnectivity of human and environmental systems becomes increasingly evident. The decisions made today will shape the human geography of tomorrow, influencing migration patterns, economic activities, and social structures. By adopting a proactive and inclusive approach to climate adaptation, societies can navigate the complexities of this changing landscape, ensuring a sustainable and equitable future for all. Engaging in international cooperation is also essential, as climate change knows no borders, and its impacts on human geography will be felt globally. Collaborative efforts to reduce greenhouse gas emissions, share adaptation strategies, and support vulnerable populations can amplify the effectiveness of individual actions. Through shared commitment and action, the global community can address the profound challenges posed by climate change and reshape human geography in ways that promote resilience, sustainability, and social justice.

Subchapter 8.3: Adaptation and Mitigation Strategies

Adaptation strategies are essential for communities to enhance their resilience against the adverse effects of climate change. These strategies can range from constructing flood barriers to implementing water conservation techniques, each tailored to address specific environmental challenges. For instance, coastal cities might focus on building sea walls and improving drainage systems to protect against rising sea levels, while agricultural communities may adopt drought-resistant crops and efficient irrigation methods to combat water scarcity. It's crucial for these adaptation measures to be integrated into local planning and development policies to ensure long-term sustainability and protection of vulnerable populations.

Mitigation strategies, on the other hand, aim to reduce the causes of climate change, primarily by lowering greenhouse gas emissions. Transitioning to renewable energy sources, such as solar and wind, plays a pivotal role in these efforts. Encouraging public transportation, cycling, and walking reduces emissions from vehicles, while energy-efficient buildings and appliances decrease overall energy consumption. Reforestation and afforestation projects not only absorb CO_2 but also restore biodiversity and improve air and water quality. Governments, businesses, and individuals all have roles to play in adopting and promoting practices that contribute to a low-carbon future.

Public engagement and education are fundamental to the success of both adaptation and mitigation efforts. Raising awareness about the impacts of climate change and the importance of taking action encourages community involvement and support for sustainability initiatives. Schools, media, and public campaigns can disseminate information on how individuals can contribute to climate resilience, from reducing energy use to participating in local environmental projects.

Innovative financing mechanisms are also critical to support the implementation of adaptation and mitigation strategies. This can include investments in green infrastructure, subsidies for renewable energy, and financial incentives for businesses and households adopting sustainable practices. International cooperation is vital, as climate change is a global issue that requires collective action. Sharing knowledge, technology, and resources across borders can enhance the effectiveness of response strategies and ensure that all countries, especially those most vulnerable to climate change, have the capacity to adapt and mitigate its impacts.

Collaboration between various stakeholders, including governments, NGOs, the private sector, and local communities, is key to developing and implementing effective adaptation and mitigation strategies. By working together, these groups can leverage their unique strengths and resources to address the complex challenges posed by climate change. This collaborative approach also ensures that strategies are inclusive and equitable, taking into consideration the needs and voices of all segments of society, particularly those who are most at risk.

Monitoring and evaluation mechanisms are crucial to assess the effectiveness of adaptation and mitigation strategies over time. This involves tracking progress, identifying challenges, and making necessary adjustments to ensure that goals are met. Data collected through these processes can provide valuable insights for future planning and decision-making, helping to refine strategies and maximize their impact.

Engaging in sustainable practices not only addresses the immediate challenges of climate change but also contributes to broader environmental, economic, and social benefits. By reducing emissions, conserving natural resources, and enhancing ecosystem resilience, societies can create healthier, more sustainable environments for current and future generations. The transition to a more sustainable world requires creativity, commitment, and concerted action from everyone. Through education, innovation, and collaboration, we can overcome the challenges of climate change and build a more resilient and sustainable future.

Chapter 9: Practice Questions and Case Studies

Delving into the realm of AP Human Geography, it's crucial to not only grasp the theoretical concepts but also to apply this knowledge through practice questions and case studies. This approach aids in solidifying your understanding and preparing you for the types of questions you'll encounter on the exam. Let's start with some practice questions that cover a variety of topics within the AP Human Geography curriculum. These questions are designed to challenge your comprehension and analytical skills, providing a comprehensive review of the material covered in previous chapters.

1. Which of the following best describes the concept of cultural diffusion

[A] The process by which population growth exceeds the carrying capacity of an area

[B] The spread of cultural beliefs and social activities from one group to another

[C] The decline in industrial activity in a region

[D] The movement of people from rural areas to cities

2. The demographic transition model explains how changes in fertility and mortality rates affect population growth. Which stage is characterized by high birth rates and high death rates

[A] Stage 1: Pre-Industrial

[B] Stage 2: Transitional

[C] Stage 3: Industrial

[D] Stage 4: Post-Industrial

3. In the context of urban geography, what does the term "urban sprawl" refer to

[A] The migration of people from urban areas to rural areas

[B] The compact, vertical growth of urban areas

[C] The unplanned and uncontrolled spreading of cities into surrounding regions

[D] The development of commercial centers on the outskirts of a city

4. Which of the following is an example of a centrifugal force in political geography

[A] A shared national language

[B] A strong sense of national pride among citizens

[C] Religious differences that lead to conflict within a state

[D] A country's centralized form of government

5. The concept of "carrying capacity" is most closely associated with which of the following

[A] Urbanization and the development of mega-cities

[B] The maximum population size an environment can sustain

[C] The diffusion of industrial practices to developing countries

[D] The transition from mercantilism to capitalism in European economies

6. What is the primary factor that drives the process of urbanization?

[A] Increased agricultural productivity

[B] Industrialization and job opportunities

[C] Natural population growth

[D] Government policies promoting rural development

7. Which of the following best describes the term "gentrification"?

[A] The process of urban decay in a neighborhood

[B] The influx of wealthier residents into a previously lower-income area

[C] The establishment of new agricultural practices in urban areas

[D] The movement of people from cities to suburbs

8. In the context of globalization, what does the term "glocalization" refer to?

[A] The complete homogenization of cultures worldwide

[B] The adaptation of global products to local markets

[C] The rejection of global influences by local cultures

[D] The isolation of local economies from global trade

9. Which of the following is a characteristic of a "megalopolis"?

[A] A small, rural community

[B] A large urban area formed by the merging of multiple cities

[C] A city with a declining population

[D] A region with no urban development

10. What is the primary purpose of a "zoning ordinance"?
[A] To regulate the types of activities that can occur in different areas
[B] To promote urban sprawl
[C] To increase property taxes in urban areas
[D] To limit the number of residents in a city

These questions serve as a primer to the types of inquiries you might face on the actual AP exam. They are crafted to test your knowledge across a broad spectrum of topics within human geography, including cultural patterns, population dynamics, urbanization, political geography, and environmental sustainability. As you work through these questions, consider the underlying concepts and how they interconnect within the broader scope of human geography. This will not only aid in answering multiple-choice questions but also in tackling free-response questions that require a deeper level of analysis and application of knowledge.

In addition to practice questions, examining case studies is an invaluable method for understanding the real-world application of human geography concepts. Case studies provide context and depth to theoretical knowledge, illustrating how geographic principles play out in actual scenarios. They can highlight the complexities and nuances of human-environment interactions, the impacts of cultural and political processes on landscapes, and the challenges and solutions in urban and rural development. By analyzing case studies, you gain insights into the multifaceted nature of geography and its relevance to contemporary issues. This approach not only enhances your comprehension of the subject matter but also equips you with the analytical skills necessary to evaluate and respond to geographic problems.

To further deepen your understanding and prepare for the AP Human Geography exam, let's explore some case studies that reflect the application of geographic concepts in real-world settings. These case studies are selected to illustrate the diversity of issues and solutions within the field of human geography, providing a practical perspective on the topics discussed in earlier chapters.

Case Study 1: Urbanization in Mega-Cities

Examine the rapid urbanization of Tokyo, Japan, one of the world's largest mega-cities. This case study explores the challenges Tokyo faces, including housing shortages, transportation congestion, and environmental pollution. It also discusses innovative solutions such as the development of vertical gardens, efficient public transportation systems, and policies aimed at reducing carbon emissions. This case highlights the importance of sustainable urban planning and the role of technology in managing the complexities of urban growth.

Case Study 2: Migration Patterns and Theories

Consider the migration crisis in the Mediterranean region, focusing on the push and pull factors that lead to the movement of people from North Africa and the Middle East to Europe. This case study delves into the geopolitical, economic, and environmental reasons behind migration flows and examines the responses of European countries to the influx of migrants and refugees. It provides insights into the human geography concepts of migration theories, barriers to migration, and the impact of migration on both origin and destination countries.

Case Study 3: Agricultural Practices and Sustainability

Explore the implementation of sustainable agriculture practices in the Brazilian Amazon. This case study addresses the challenges of deforestation, biodiversity loss, and climate change. It showcases the adoption of agroforestry, organic farming, and other sustainable practices that aim to preserve the Amazon's ecological balance while providing economic benefits to local communities. This example underscores the significance of environmental sustainability in agricultural development and the role of local and global efforts in conserving natural resources.

Case Study 4: Cultural Landscapes and Identity

Investigate the preservation of cultural landscapes in Bali, Indonesia, where traditional rice terraces (Subak) play a crucial role in the island's cultural and religious identity. This case study examines the impact of tourism and modernization on Bali's cultural landscapes and discusses initiatives to protect and maintain these areas as symbols of cultural heritage. It illustrates the concept of cultural landscapes as dynamic entities shaped by human-environment interactions and the importance of cultural preservation in the face of globalization.

Case Study 5: Climate Change Adaptation and Mitigation

Analyze the strategies employed by the Netherlands to combat the effects of climate change, particularly sea-level rise. This case study highlights the country's innovative approaches to water management, including the construction of barriers, dykes, and artificial islands, as well as policies aimed at reducing greenhouse gas emissions. It demonstrates how geographic concepts of human-environment interaction and sustainability are applied in developing adaptation and mitigation strategies to address climate change.

Through these case studies, you can see how the principles of human geography are applied to solve complex problems in diverse settings around the world. By examining these real-world examples, you gain a deeper appreciation of the relevance of geographic concepts to everyday life and global challenges. As you prepare for the AP Human Geography exam, remember that understanding both the theoretical aspects and practical applications of geography will enhance your ability to analyze, evaluate, and propose solutions to geographic issues. Keep exploring, questioning, and connecting the dots between human activities and the geographic environment, and you'll be well on your way to mastering the fascinating field of human geography.

• *Subchapter 9.1: Exam-Style Multiple Choice*

Comprehension

1. Which of the following best describes a formal region?

A. An area with undefined boundaries based on cultural perceptions.

B. A space defined by uniform political or cultural traits.

C. A region organized around a chemical fallout shelter.

D. An area where people share similar economic activities.

The correct answer is B.

Understanding formal regions is crucial in human geography, as they help us categorize and analyze areas based on specific characteristics that are consistent throughout. This knowledge not only aids in academic success but also enhances our comprehension of the world around us.

Analysis

2. Analyze the impact of remote sensing technology on geographic data collection. Which statement most accurately reflects this impact?

A. Remote sensing has increased the reliance on manual data collection methods.

B. It has limited the ability to monitor environmental changes over time.

C. Remote sensing provides real-time data, enhancing the accuracy of geographic analyses.

D. The technology is only useful for urban area studies.

The correct answer is C.

Understanding the role of remote sensing technology is essential for grasping how geographic data is collected and utilized. This technology revolutionizes the way we observe and analyze our environment, allowing for timely and precise assessments of changes in land use, vegetation, and climate patterns. By leveraging remote sensing, geographers can make informed decisions that impact urban planning, environmental management, and disaster response, ultimately leading to a more sustainable and well-informed approach to geographic studies.

Application

3. A city planner is using Geographic Information Systems (GIS) to optimize public transportation routes. Which application of GIS would most effectively achieve this goal?

A. Mapping historical migration patterns to predict future population changes.

B. Analyzing traffic density data to identify areas with the highest demand for bus services.

C. Studying cultural landscapes to enhance tourist attractions.

D. Evaluating climate change data to plan for future environmental policies.

The correct answer is B.

Analyzing traffic density data is crucial for city planners as it allows them to pinpoint where the demand for public transportation is greatest. By focusing on areas with high traffic density, planners can make informed decisions about where to allocate resources, improve service frequency, and ultimately enhance the efficiency of public transportation systems. This application of GIS not only optimizes routes but also contributes to a more sustainable urban environment by encouraging the use of public transit over personal vehicles.

• Subchapter 9.2: Free Response Questions (FRQ) Practice

Comprehension

1. Describe the concept of cultural landscapes and explain how they reflect the relationship between human activities and the natural environment.

Analysis

2. Analyze the impact of globalization on local economies. Discuss both positive and negative effects with specific geographic examples.

Application

3. Using population distribution theories, evaluate the potential challenges a rapidly growing city might face in managing its resources and infrastructure.

Structuring High-Scoring FRQs

Crafting high-scoring Free Response Questions (FRQs) for the AP Human Geography exam requires a strategic approach that demonstrates not only your understanding of the content but also your ability to apply this knowledge critically and coherently. To excel in FRQs, it's essential to structure your responses in a way that directly addresses the question's requirements while showcasing your depth of understanding and analytical skills. Here are some actionable steps and strategies to guide you in structuring FRQs that can earn you top marks.

Firstly, carefully read the FRQ prompt to grasp fully what it asks. Identify the key components of the question and any specific geographic concepts or terms it mentions. This initial step is crucial as it sets the direction for your entire response. Highlight or underline significant words or phrases in the prompt to ensure that you address each part of the question.

Begin your response with a clear and concise introduction that outlines your understanding of the question and briefly states the points you plan to discuss. This introduction sets the tone for your answer and helps the examiner see that you have a clear grasp of the task at hand.

For each main point you make, start with a topic sentence that introduces the idea or argument you will discuss. This sentence should directly relate to the question and the information you outlined in your introduction. Following the topic sentence, provide detailed explanations, examples, and evidence that support your point. Use specific geographic terms and concepts you've learned, and whenever possible, include real-world examples that illustrate your points. This not only demonstrates your knowledge but also your ability to apply theoretical concepts to practical situations.

Incorporate diagrams, maps, or charts if the question lends itself to a visual representation and if time allows. Visual aids can enhance your response by providing a clear, concise way to demonstrate complex geographic concepts or data. Ensure that any visual element you include is well-labeled and directly relevant to your argument.

Critical analysis is a vital component of high-scoring FRQs. Where appropriate, analyze the implications, challenges, or significance of the concepts you are discussing. This could involve evaluating the effectiveness of different geographic models, discussing the potential impacts of a phenomenon, or comparing and contrasting geographic theories. Showing your ability to think critically about the material not only reinforces your understanding but also demonstrates higher-level thinking skills that are rewarded in the scoring of FRQs.

Conclude each section of your response by summarizing the main points you've made and linking them back to the question. This helps to reinforce your arguments and ensures that your response is cohesive and focused.

Time management is crucial when tackling FRQs. Practice structuring your responses within the time limits of the exam to ensure that you can thoroughly address each part of the question without running out of time. It can be helpful to allocate a specific amount of time to planning, writing, and reviewing your response to ensure clarity and completeness.

Lastly, practice is key to mastering the structure of high-scoring FRQs. Regularly practice with past AP Human Geography FRQs, applying these strategies to a variety of question types and topics. Seek feedback on your practice responses to identify areas for improvement and refine your approach.

By following these strategies and dedicating time to practice, you can develop the skills necessary to structure compelling, comprehensive FRQ responses. This will not only aid in your success on the AP Human Geography exam but also enhance your overall geographic literacy and analytical abilities.

Subchapter 9.3: Common Pitfalls and Mistakes to Avoid

Avoiding common pitfalls and mistakes is crucial for excelling in the AP® Human Geography exam. Students often fall into traps that hinder their performance, not because of a lack of knowledge, but due to poor exam strategies or misconceptions about the test itself. Recognizing these pitfalls is the first step toward overcoming them.

Firstly, **overlooking the importance of practice questions** is a mistake many students make. The AP® exam format can be challenging, and familiarity with the types of questions asked is essential. Engaging regularly with practice questions, especially those that mimic the exam format, builds confidence and helps identify areas needing further review.

Misunderstanding the Free Response Questions (FRQs) is another common error. Students sometimes focus solely on content knowledge, neglecting the importance of structuring their answers effectively. Each FRQ should be approached with a clear structure in mind: introduction, main points with evidence, and a concise conclusion. Practicing this structure can significantly improve scores.

Neglecting the exam's time constraints can severely impact performance. Some students spend too much time on difficult questions, leaving insufficient time for others. A balanced approach, allocating time based on the point value of each question, is advisable. If a question seems too challenging, it's better to move on and return to it later if time allows.

Underestimating the importance of key terms and concepts is a pitfall that can easily be avoided. The AP® Human Geography exam requires a deep understanding of specific terminology and concepts. Flashcards, glossaries, and regular review sessions can be invaluable tools for mastering this aspect of the exam.

Failing to apply concepts to real-world scenarios is a mistake that can cost valuable points. The AP® Human Geography exam often asks students to apply theoretical knowledge to practical examples. Regularly practicing this skill, by relating concepts to current events or personal observations, can enhance the ability to think critically under exam conditions.

Ignoring the value of peer study groups can also be detrimental. Studying in groups can provide new insights, reinforce learning through teaching, and offer moral support. However, it's important to ensure that study sessions remain focused and productive.

Over-reliance on memorization rather than understanding is a common trap. While memorization of key facts and figures is necessary, the ability to analyze, compare, and contrast different geographic concepts is what truly demonstrates mastery of the subject.

Neglecting self-care in the lead-up to the exam can impair cognitive function and overall performance. Adequate sleep, nutrition, and exercise are all critical for peak performance. It's also important to manage stress through relaxation techniques or leisure activities.

By being aware of these common pitfalls and actively working to avoid them, students can improve their chances of achieving a high score on the AP® Human Geography exam. Regular practice, effective time management, and a focus on understanding over memorization are key strategies for success.

Chapter 10: Exam Strategy and Time Management

In the realm of AP® Human Geography, mastering time management during the exam is as crucial as understanding the content itself. The key to effectively navigating this challenge lies in developing a strategic approach to both study and exam execution.

One effective strategy is to allocate specific time blocks to different sections of the exam, ensuring that each question receives the attention it deserves without compromising the time available for others. For instance, dedicating approximately one minute per multiple-choice question allows for a thorough review while maintaining a steady pace. To practice this, you can set a timer for 60 minutes and attempt a set of 60 multiple-choice questions. After completing the questions, review your answers and note the time taken for each question to identify any patterns in your pacing.

Similarly, for the Free Response Questions (FRQs), breaking down the allotted time into segments for planning, writing, and reviewing can significantly enhance the quality of responses. A suggested approach is to allocate 10 minutes for planning, 20 minutes for writing, and 5 minutes for reviewing each FRQ. To implement this, practice with a sample FRQ: first, read the prompt and outline your response in 10 minutes. Then, write your answer in 20 minutes, focusing on clarity and structure. Finally, use the last 5 minutes to read through your response, checking for any errors or areas for improvement.

Another pivotal aspect of time management is the prioritization of study topics based on their weight in the exam and personal strengths and weaknesses. Create a study schedule that allocates more time to challenging topics while ensuring that you revisit all areas regularly. For example, if you find urban geography difficult, dedicate extra study sessions to that topic while still reviewing other areas like population geography.

Practice exams play a crucial role in this strategy, offering a realistic gauge of where time management adjustments are necessary and helping to familiarize students with the exam's format and pacing. After taking a practice exam, analyze your results to see which sections took longer than expected and adjust your study plan accordingly.

Review sessions should be strategically placed in the study schedule to reinforce learning and ensure retention of information. These sessions are most effective when they involve active recall practices, such as teaching the material to someone else or applying concepts to different scenarios, rather than passive review methods. For instance, after studying a topic, try to explain it to a friend or family member, or create flashcards with key terms and concepts to test yourself.

Incorporating breaks into the study schedule is also vital for maintaining mental stamina and preventing burnout. Short, frequent breaks can help to refresh the mind and improve concentration over long study sessions. During these breaks, engaging in physical activity or other forms of relaxation can help to clear the mind and reduce stress. Consider using the Pomodoro Technique: study for 25 minutes, then take a 5-minute break. After four cycles, take a longer break of 15-30 minutes.

The night before the exam, it's imperative to prioritize rest over last-minute cramming. A well-rested brain performs significantly better in terms of memory recall, critical thinking, and problem-solving. Preparing all necessary materials ahead of time and ensuring a good night's sleep can set the stage for optimal performance on exam day. Aim for at least 7-8 hours of sleep to ensure you wake up refreshed and ready to tackle the exam.

On the day of the exam, maintaining a positive mindset and employing relaxation techniques can help to alleviate anxiety and improve focus. Techniques such as deep breathing or visualization can be effective. For example, take a few moments to close your eyes, breathe deeply, and visualize yourself confidently answering questions. Approaching the exam with confidence, grounded in thorough preparation and a clear strategy for time management, can make a significant difference in the outcome.

By adhering to these strategies, students can enhance their ability to manage time effectively, both in preparation for and during the AP® Human Geography exam. This disciplined approach not only aids in mastering the exam content but also in developing skills that are valuable far beyond the exam room.

Subchapter 10.1: Allocating Time for Each Section

Allocating time for each section of the AP® Human Geography exam requires a strategic approach to ensure that every question, whether multiple-choice or free-response, is given adequate attention. The exam is structured to test not only your knowledge of human geography but also your ability to manage time effectively under pressure. To excel, it's crucial to understand the breakdown of the exam and how to distribute your time across its components. The multiple-choice section, comprising 60 questions, is to be completed in 60 minutes, which translates to about one minute per question. This rapid pace demands quick reading and decision-making skills. It's advisable to first answer questions you're confident about to secure those points early on. If a question seems too complex or time-consuming, mark it and move on, returning to it only after addressing the more straightforward questions.

For the free-response section, you have 75 minutes to answer three questions. This gives you roughly 25 minutes per question, but it's wise to allocate this time unevenly based on your strengths and the complexity of each question. Spend the first few minutes planning your answers, jotting down key points, and organizing your thoughts to ensure a coherent and comprehensive response. Aim to spend no more than 20 minutes writing each answer, reserving the last few minutes for reviewing and refining your responses. This review time can be critical for catching and correcting any mistakes or for adding any additional points that can bolster your argument.

Practicing with timed exams can greatly improve your time management skills. By simulating exam conditions, you can identify which sections or types of questions slow you down and adjust your strategy accordingly. It's also beneficial to practice pacing yourself without a clock in direct view, as this mirrors the actual exam setting and helps build an internal sense of timing.

Remember, the goal is not just to answer all the questions within the allotted time but to do so with the clarity and depth that high-scoring responses require. Balancing speed with thoroughness is key. As you practice, you'll find the right rhythm and approach that works best for you, allowing you to enter the exam room with confidence in your ability to manage your time effectively and perform at your best.

Subchapter 10.2: Last-Minute Study Tips

In the final hours before the AP® Human Geography exam, it's natural to feel a mix of anticipation and anxiety. However, this time can be used effectively to boost confidence and readiness. **Focus on light review** rather than trying to cram new information. Revisit key terms, concepts, and case studies that have been challenging in the past. This is not the moment for deep dives into unfamiliar material but for reinforcing what you already know.

Organize your study materials so that everything you might need for a quick review is at your fingertips. This could include flashcards, summary notes, or a list of key terms. The goal is to make this process as efficient as possible, minimizing stress and maximizing recall.

Practice relaxation techniques to manage exam anxiety. Techniques such as deep breathing, visualization, or even a short walk can help clear your mind and reduce stress. Remember, a calm mind is more capable of recalling information than one clouded by anxiety.

Ensure you have all necessary materials ready for the exam day. Check the requirements for the test center and prepare your bag with essentials such as pencils, an eraser, a calculator (if allowed), and your ID. Avoiding last-minute scrambles for these items can help maintain a calm state of mind.

Set a clear plan for the exam day including when to wake up, what to eat for breakfast, and how to get to the test center. A predictable routine can help ease nerves and set a positive tone for the day.

Get a good night's sleep before the exam. While it might be tempting to stay up late for last-minute studying, the benefits of being well-rested cannot be overstated. Sleep enhances memory recall and cognitive function, both critical for exam success.

Stay hydrated and eat a nutritious meal before the exam. Proper nutrition can have a significant impact on your energy levels and concentration. Avoid heavy, greasy foods that might make you feel sluggish and opt for something light but sustaining.

Review the exam format one last time to ensure you're clear on the structure and types of questions you'll be facing. This can help reduce surprises and build confidence.

Set realistic expectations for the exam. While it's important to aim high, remember that perfection is not the goal. Focus on doing your best and remember that there are multiple pathways to your academic and career goals, regardless of this single exam outcome.

By following these last-minute study tips, you can approach the AP® Human Geography exam with a sense of preparedness and calm. Remember, you've already put in the hard work. Now it's time to trust in your preparation and give it your best shot.

Subchapter 10.3: Exam Day Tips and Strategies

Arriving at the exam location early is a strategy that cannot be overstated. This allows you time to settle in, familiarize yourself with the surroundings, and mentally prepare for the task ahead. It's advisable to aim for at least 30 minutes before the scheduled start time. This buffer can help mitigate any unforeseen delays and reduce pre-exam stress. Once seated, take a moment to organize your workspace. Lay out your pencils, eraser, and any other permitted materials neatly. This small act of preparation can have a calming effect, putting you in the right mindset for the exam.

Before the exam begins, take several deep breaths to center yourself. Deep breathing exercises can be remarkably effective in lowering your heart rate and calming nerves. Remember, you've prepared for this moment, and you have the tools and knowledge needed to succeed.

As the exam starts, carefully read through all instructions. Misreading directions under pressure is common, but taking a few extra seconds to understand what is being asked can save you from making avoidable errors. For the multiple-choice section, if you encounter a question that stumps you, don't linger too long. Instead, mark it and move on. You can always return to it later with fresh eyes. This approach ensures that you don't waste precious time on a single question, allowing you to address each question on the exam.

For the free-response section, outline your answers before diving into writing. A brief outline can help organize your thoughts and ensure your response is coherent and comprehensive. Start with the questions you feel most confident about to build momentum. If you find yourself stuck on a particular point, move on and come back to it later. Often, working on other parts of the exam can jog your memory or inspire a new angle on a challenging question.

Throughout the exam, keep an eye on the clock, but try not to check it obsessively. Allocate your time wisely, but also allow for flexibility. If you've dedicated too much time to one section, adjust your strategy for the remaining questions. Time management is about finding a balance between speed and accuracy.

If you finish early, use the remaining time to review your answers, especially in sections where you felt uncertain. Double-check your work for careless mistakes or omitted answers. However, avoid second-guessing yourself too much; often, your first instinct is correct.

Maintaining a positive attitude throughout the exam is crucial. Remind yourself of your preparation and the hard work you've put in. Confidence can significantly impact your performance, so focus on your strengths and the progress you've made in your studies.

Finally, after the exam, take time to decompress and reflect on the experience. Consider what strategies worked well and what you might adjust for future exams. Regardless of the outcome, remember that this exam is just one step in your academic journey. Each challenge is an opportunity to learn and grow, preparing you for whatever comes next.

Appendix

The appendix serves as a vital resource for students aiming to excel in the AP® Human Geography exam. It includes a glossary of key terms that are essential for understanding the core concepts discussed throughout this guide. These terms have been carefully selected to cover a broad spectrum of topics within human geography, ensuring students are well-prepared for the exam.

- **Absolute Location**: The precise geographical position of a place or feature on the Earth's surface.
- **Birth Rate**: The number of live births per 1,000 people in a population in a given year.
- **Cultural Diffusion**: The spread of cultural beliefs and social activities from one group to another.
- **Demographic Transition Model**: A model that describes population change over time.
- **Economic Development**: The process by which the economic well-being and quality of life of a nation, region, or local community are improved.
- **Fertility Rate**: The average number of children born to a woman over her lifetime.
- **Gentrification**: The process of renovating and improving a house or district so that it conforms to middle-class taste.
- **Human Geography**: The branch of geography dealing with how human activity affects or is influenced by the Earth's surface.
- **Infrastructure**: The basic physical and organizational structures and facilities needed for the operation of a society or enterprise.
- **Jurisdiction**: The official power to make legal decisions and judgments.
- **Kinship**: The blood relationship between people.
- **Land Use**: The management and modification of natural environment or wilderness into built environment such as settlements and semi-natural habitats such as arable fields, pastures, and managed woods.

- **Migration**: The movement of people from one place to another with the intentions of settling, permanently or temporarily, at a new location.
- **Nonrenewable Resources**: Natural resources that cannot be replaced at the same rate at which they are consumed.
- **Outsourcing**: Obtain (goods or a service) from an outside or foreign supplier, especially in place of an internal source.
- **Population Density**: The number of people living per unit of an area; the number of people relative to the space occupied by them.
- **Quota**: A limited quantity of a particular product that under official controls can be produced, exported, or imported.
- **Renewable Resources**: Resources that are naturally replenished on a human timescale.
- **Sustainability**: The ability to be maintained at a certain rate or level.
- **Territory**: An area of land under the jurisdiction of a ruler or state.
- **Urbanization**: The process by which towns and cities are formed and become larger as more people begin living and working in central areas.
- **Vernacular Region**: An area that people believe exists as part of their cultural identity.
- **Watershed**: An area or ridge of land that separates waters flowing to different rivers, basins, or seas.
- **Xenophobia**: Dislike of or prejudice against people from other countries.
- **Youth Dependency Ratio**: A measure showing the ratio of the number of individuals aged 0-14 to the number of individuals aged 15-64 in a given country.
- **Zero Population Growth**: A condition of demographic balance where the number of people in a specified population neither grows nor declines.

This glossary is designed to be a quick reference tool, aiding students in their study sessions and providing a comprehensive overview of the terminology that forms the foundation of the AP® Human Geography curriculum.

Glossary of Key Terms

- **Urban Sprawl**: The expansion of urban areas into the surrounding rural areas, often characterized by low-density residential development, dependence on cars, and lack of public transportation options. It is associated with various environmental and social issues, including increased pollution and loss of wildlife habitats.
- **Supranational Organizations**: Entities formed by three or more states to promote shared objectives. Examples include the European Union (EU) and the United Nations (UN). These organizations play crucial roles in geopolitical conflicts, economic policies, and environmental conservation efforts.
- **Sovereignty**: The authority of a state to govern itself or another state. It is a key concept in political geography, affecting international relations, border disputes, and the creation of new countries.
- **Renewable Energy**: Energy from sources that are naturally replenishing but flow-limited. Renewable resources are virtually inexhaustible in duration but limited in the amount of energy available per unit of time. Examples include solar, wind, and hydroelectric power.
- **Push and Pull Factors**: In migration theory, push factors are those that force an individual to move away from a location, while pull factors are those that attract an individual to a new location. These factors can include economic, social, political, and environmental conditions.
- **Primary, Secondary, Tertiary Economic Sectors**: The primary sector involves the extraction of raw materials, the secondary sector involves manufacturing, and the tertiary sector involves services. Understanding the distribution of these sectors is crucial for analyzing economic development and industrialization patterns.
- **GIS (Geographic Information Systems)**: A framework for gathering, managing, and analyzing data rooted in the science of geography. GIS integrates many types of data and is used in various fields, including urban planning, environmental management, and emergency response.
- **Cultural Landscape**: An area fashioned from nature by a cultural group. This concept encompasses both physical structures and the cultural practices that shape the landscape. It is a key concept in understanding how humans interact with their environment.

- **Biodiversity Conservation**: The practice of protecting and preserving the variety of life forms on Earth, including different species, ecosystems, and genetic diversity. Biodiversity conservation is critical for maintaining ecosystem services and resilience.

Bonus For You

Answers

Subchapter 2.2: Population Distribution and Density

1. [D] Color of the land

2. [B] Total population / Total area

3. [B] River valley

4. [B] Industrialization

5. [D] All of the above

6. [B] High levels of pollution

7. [C] Housing shortages

8. [C] Arid deserts

9. [B] Outmigration

10. [B] Total population / Total area

Subchapter 2.3: Migration Patterns and Theories

1. [D] Lee's Model of Migration

2. [C] A worker relocating to a city where relatives already reside

3. [B] High crime rates in the home country

4. [C] Circular migration

5. [A] Money sent back home by migrants

6. [B] Job opportunities

7. [B] Urbanization

8. [A] Distance and population size

9. [C] A refugee fleeing a war zone

10. [B] The emigration of highly educated individuals

Push and Pull Factors

1. [B] High levels of pollution

2. [B] Destination for immigration due to pull factors

3. [C] Migration is often the result of a combination of push and pull factors

4. [C] Job opportunities

5. [B] Push factors

6. [B] Political persecution

7. [B] Destination for immigration due to pull factors

8. [A] Push factors

9. [B] Availability of affordable housing

10. [B] Pull factors

Case Studies of Migration: Historical & Modern

1. [A] The availability of industrial jobs in the North

2. [C] A forced migration due to economic and political instability

3. [B] By showing the effects of migration on urban and rural landscapes

4. [B] Increased cultural diversity and the establishment of vibrant communitie

5. [B] Families fleeing violence and economic hardship

6. [B] It caused economic hardship for Southern farmers

7. [B] Colombia

8. [A] Decreased job opportunities for locals

9. [B] It contributed to the Harlem Renaissance

10. [C] Economic hardship

Chapter 3: Cultural Patterns and Processes

1. [B] Terraced agricultural fields in mountainous regions

2. [B] Through the design of spaces that facilitate social interaction and community events

3. [C] They influence behavior, social interactions, and the organization of society

4. [B] Traditional music and dance specific to a local community

5. [B] They create opportunities for cultural exchange and hybridization

6. [A] Geographic location

7. [B] Rapid spread of cultural traits through direct contact

8. [B] They reinforce social norms and community bonds

9. [B] The introduction of a new fashion trend from a major city to smaller towns

10. [B] They showcase the wealth and resources of a society

Subchapter 3.1: Cultural Landscapes and Identity

1. [B] Town on trade route

2. [B] Mirrors and influences cultural practices

3. [B] Support local artisans with traditional methods

4. [B] They foster a sense of belonging and pride

5. [B] Loss of historical and cultural significance

6. [B] Created with specific aesthetic goals

7. [B] It promotes cultural blending

8. [B] Supporting indigenous languages

9. [C] Loss of unique cultural identities

10. [B] They symbolize shared beliefs and practices

Chapter 9: PracticeQuestions and Case Studies

1. [B] The spread of cultural beliefs and social activities from one group to another

2. [A] Stage 1: Pre-Industrial

3. [C] The unplanned and uncontrolled spreading of cities into surrounding regions

4. [C] Religious differences that lead to conflict within a state**

5. [B] The maximum population size an environment can sustain

6. [B] Industrialization and job opportunities

7. [B] The influx of wealthier residents into a previously lower-income area

8. [B] The adaptation of global products to local markets

9. [B] A large urban area formed by the merging of multiple cities

10. [A] To regulate the types of activities that can occur in different areas

Made in United States
Troutdale, OR
04/08/2025